Back Alley Reporter

Back Alley Reporter

Mike McCardell

HARBOUR PUBLISHING

HARBOUR PUBLISHING CO. LTD.
P.O. Box 219
Madeira Park, BC, V0N 2H0
Canada
www.harbourpublishing.com

Cover photographs of Mike McCardell by Nick Didlick
Printed and bound in Canada

THE CANADA COUNCIL | LE CONSEIL DES ARTS
FOR THE ARTS | DU CANADA
SINCE 1957 | DEPUIS 1957

BRITISH
COLUMBIA
ARTS COUNCIL
We acknowledge the support of the Province of British Columbia
through the British Columbia Arts Council

Harbour Publishing acknowledges financial support from the Government of Canada
through the Canada Council for the Arts and the Book Publishing Industry Development
Program (BPIDP), and from the Province of British Columbia through the British Columbia
Arts Council, for its publishing activities.

LIBRARY AND ARCHIVES CANADA CATALOGUING IN PUBLICATION

McCardell, Mike, 1944-
    Back alley reporter / Mike McCardell.

ISBN 978-1-55017-480-9

    1. McCardell, Mike, 1944-. I. Title.
PN4913.M36A3 2009   C818'.602   C2008-907917-5

To Colleen and Sean
Now it is my turn to look up to both of you.

CONTENTS

Preface

This book is written in the belief that a good life has nothing to do with wealth or luck. Those who enjoy being alive simply want it that way, work for it, imagine it, search for it and then they usually get it. It does not require a pretty face, a fat wallet or a university degree, only the desire and determination to do something good with the only thing we temporarily have, life.

I did not create these stories. I only reported them. It is the people—so many thousands of them that the stories are about—that I owe my job and my memories to, as well as my livelihood. You have made my life a pleasure. Thank you.

But I would like to give a medal to a few individuals, for being my friends and for sharing my stories and sharing their lives with me:

Avrille and Mike Hewett. We have stood on different sides of the fence of politics, social reform and language (they are English), but we have still laughed together and stuck together.

Freda and George Ellis, who are city folks but want to live like cow punchers on the open range of the Cariboo.

Their biffy inspired the closing words in this book. It is a reader's paradise.

Ingrid Rice and Bob York, who live in left field and enjoy being there. She is an editorial cartoonist known across Canada. Bob is a musician who should be in the Philharmonic, but plays at old folks' homes. They also raise guinea pigs, which have taken over their house, their lawn and their lives. If you are in their company and you are dull, you are dead.

And Ruth Olde and Gunther Blasig, who are landscapers of both the earth and those who walk on it. They have turned weed-choked lots into gardens of beauty, but more importantly they have brightened lives by cultivating friendships that have a chance to grow like nourished gardens.

And Mary Schendlinger, the finest editor I have known since I left a big-city newspaper in New York. She is magical with words, and like all good editors she makes the writer look good without taking credit herself. If we all had an editor as good as Mary, the world would be much easier to understand, and not just for its writing.

THE SWIMMING HOLE

"My mother says it's hot, but it's not really hot. Hot is in the desert where it gets to be 110 degrees." Johnny Martin was explaining his perception of hot while sweat dripped down his face. He had no idea what a desert was, but if his mother said this was hot, Johnny would say it wasn't. After all, his mother was an adult.

It was July. We could feel the burning street through the bottoms of our sneakers. But we weren't going to admit that it was hot. Hot was an adult condition. If they said it was hot then we would say no, we liked it this way.

"What sweat?" we would say. "I'm not sweating. I don't feel a thing."

But that didn't stop the asphalt under our feet from getting soft. It didn't stop the old men sitting on the steps in front of their houses from wiping their hairless heads with wet handkerchiefs or young mothers from fanning their babies who were screaming in hot carriages.

The walls inside our homes and apartments were as warm as the outside of a toaster. But it didn't matter.

"I feel fine," said Dorothy to her grandfather. "You may be hot, but I like this."

It was even better to disagree with grandparents than with parents because grandparents would eventually agree with you and then you would have two or three against your parents, which was a winning combination.

But now that we were out on the street away from our parents, and the sun was burning the paint off the buildings and there were no trees to soak up the heat, it was OK to admit that we were frying.

"We got to go swimming," said Tommy.

Tommy knew how to give orders. Tommy's father had been in the Navy and he gave orders at home, so when Tommy went out on the street he gave orders to the other kids. Since none of us had any ideas about what we wanted to do, we were willing to follow any order to do anything.

Once in the pond we would be cool. We would dive in and leave the sun behind. It was beautiful down there, far below the surface. We could twist and turn and pretend we were fish. No adults yelled at us and we had no cares and no worries, and we did not even get wet.

Our pond was a two-minute walk around the corner from our street. It appeared only in the summer because that was when the ice cream factory was working around the clock, with trucks coming and going and unloading box after box of sugar and paper wrappings and millions of wooden sticks. The boxes were tossed into an area behind a chain-link fence that went from the ground up to the roof of the factory. The boxes weren't flattened because ecology was not an issue back then.

Can you imagine the delight of an eight- or nine- or ten-year-old standing on the sidewalk and looking up at a mountain of cardboard two storeys high? It was an invitation with an open door.

"Last one up is a monkey," said Tommy. And seven kids all wearing the same summer uniform of dirty white tee shirts, jeans with holes in the knees, and sneakers bought on sale would fly up that fence with hands and feet, defying gravity, because none of us wanted to be a monkey. But we knew we were safe because Buster would be the last one. He was eight. His parents were from Armenia, and although none of us knew where that was, we knew that Buster could speak two languages and that made him smarter than all of us. But he was also smaller. So when we got to the top and slid onto the hot tar roof of the factory, we looked down at Buster and said, "Monkey, monkey."

"I'll get you," he yelled as his little legs and arms struggled up the fence. And when he climbed onto the roof he attacked everyone. No one was too big for Buster. He would punch and push, and Joey would pick him up and hold him at arm's length while Buster's fists swung through the air and we all laughed, including Buster because we all belonged together.

From the edge of the roof we could dive down into the boxes. This was perfect city swimming, because none of us actually knew how to swim, because none of us had ever been to a swimming pool. But in here you could breathe under water and you could swim down and get lost in the boxes and pretend you were exploring the bottom of the ocean. Sometimes a kid would not surface for a long time, which told us that he had found a sunken treasure. Usually it was the chocolate wafers that were used to make ice cream sandwiches, and when a box of them got broken and couldn't be used in the factory, they were thrown out. A lucky swimmer would find them tucked away among the hundreds of boxes and stuff wafers in his mouth until he was aching with thirst and ready to be sick. But he had to eat quietly, because even with the noise of the trucks and the trains across the street, kids' ears are made to pick out the sound of chocolate wafers being crunched.

"I hear eating," said Joey, who was the best swimmer. Joey was good at a lot of things that required being strong because his younger brother had cerebral palsy and Joey had to help carry him. The brother would flail his arms around and Joey learned to duck so he wouldn't get punched. Hence Joey also became a very good fighter, which was an important skill in our neighbourhood.

But now Joey's ears were working like sonar and he heard eating. He became a submarine hunting for the enemy who was Jimmy Lee, who was really his best friend, except when it came to chocolate wafers. Jimmy had them stuffed in both cheeks and in his pockets and tried to take two handfuls when he heard Joey coming, but you cannot swim with chocolate wafers in your hands.

Other swimmers wiggled through the boxes following Joey, who saw Jimmy's feet escaping. Joey grabbed the feet and pulled Jimmy back and they wrestled as vigorously as they could with a storey and a half of boxes on top of them. The wafers fell out of Jimmy's pockets and crumbled out of his hands and the rest of us swam underneath him like guppies grabbing falling food.

"Hey, you. This place is ours."

Even inside the cardboard we could hear the shouts. There was cursing and pounding on the wire mesh fence. We crawled our way toward it and there on the other side was a gang from two blocks away. Back then every neighbourhood was like a medieval fiefdom. You were OK if you stayed on your street but one block away was trouble. We always figured the factory was ours because it was on our side of the tracks. This other gang thought differently. They were also a few years older.

We had no doubt about what we would do. There was no fear, no worry. We climbed out through the opening in the side and by the time two of us were on the sidewalk the fight had begun. There was punching and kicking, and as more of us spilled out of the boxes the brawl got larger, with knees and elbows flying and with yelling and cursing and rolling on the ground. Buster was there with us, getting kicked out of the fighting and then running right back in like a junkyard cat up against dogs.

"Stop it, stop it!" It was a loud voice, and when we looked up we saw a factory worker standing over us. He was big. Even in the steaming heat of the day he wore a heavy winter parka and heavy padded pants and thick boots. A curved ice pick hung around his neck. He worked in the freezer and he was Greek, like all the workers in the factory, and because of his accent, we could only half understand him.

But we understood "Stop," in a voice that came from under a huge drooping moustache below dark eyes and darker eyebrows. He could have spoken in any language and his meaning would be clear. "No fighting," he said. "You race. The winner stays here. Loser goes away."

"We don't want to race," said one of the intruding kids. "You don't own this place. This is a free country."

The Greek stared down at the kid. "You race or I fix you so you don't race ever again."

He told us to pick one kid each and he would meet us on the roof. Then he went back inside the factory. We picked Joey and they picked Rocco, who was bigger than Joey and looked much stronger.

"What do we do now?" Rocco said.

"You climb the fence," came a voice from above. It was the Greek standing on the roof. "You," he pointed at Rocco, "you come up this end. You," he pointed at Joey, "you come up there. You go down in the boxes, you come up. The first one up can stay here."

The two boys climbed up on opposite sides of the enclosure. At the top, without even getting onto the roof, the Greek said, "Go!" and they rolled over the top of the fence and into the cardboard. They slipped and clawed at the boxes and went down with amazing speed. But it was obvious Rocco was moving faster than Joey. He was slipping through the brown ocean with ease and he reached the bottom before Joey was halfway down. We were watching our best losing before the race was half finished.

The other gang was laughing and spitting on the sidewalk in front of us, already marking the territory. But then something happened. Rocco began yelling and cursing. He wasn't moving up. He pulled himself up on some boxes, then slid back down. Joey had reached bottom and was slowly, steadily gaining on him, then passing him. It was hard to go straight up, but Joey was doing it

18

and he was halfway up when Rocco was still barely off the ground.

"It's not fair," Rocco was shouting. But we were cheering Joey so loudly that it was hard to hear the complaints.

Joey reached the top and we cheered and shouted louder and the factory worker in his white parka with the hood pushed back raised Joey's hand. "The winner," he said. He took Joey with him through an open skylight and down a ladder, and the two of them walked out the factory door together. It was the first time any of us had been inside the factory.

Rocco crawled out of the boxes through the opening in the fence. He was covered with liquid chocolate.

"It's not fair. It was too slippery," he said. "I want to do it again."

The worker pointed his finger at Rocco, and then pointed his finger toward the end of the street.

"You can't make us go," said Rocco.

The worker took his ice pick from his neck and gestured again. "You go," he said. "And you don't come back."

They took the suggestion.

Then, without a word, without an explanation, the man in the winter coat went back through the door and back to work in the freezer making ice cream. And we climbed back on the roof. And up there we saw, right where this hard-working immigrant had been standing, an empty five-gallon can of chocolate syrup. We sat on the hot tar roof and spent the next hour scraping our fingers around the inside of the can and licking off the chocolate and talking about what obviously had happened. We had a friend, and we didn't know his name.

After that we called that mountain of cardboard the Greek's Ocean.

At the end of summer the factory closed up and the workers got laid off until the next year and the boxes disappeared. But that winter in school we learned where Greece was, and after that we renamed our ocean. We spent the rest of the school year telling the other kids that next summer we would be swimming in the Mediterranean.

SpeciAl EffEcTs

In a world that was basic grey highlighted with soot, the ice cream factory was a magical place. Most of the other factories surrounding our neighbourhood made things like barbed wire and car bumpers, and they had noisy trucks parked outside. Every morning, workers would walk down our street looking down at the sidewalk and carrying lunch boxes on their way to those factories.

On the other hand, there was also the Ex-Lax factory. That was our second favourite place because the walls of it, which went right to the edge of the sidewalk, were painted chocolate brown, and when we passed it we always made the same joke and tried to push each other into the walls.

"Yuck, poo. You know what comes out of there."

We laughed and hit each other and laughed some more. This was in an age before profanity. It is hard to believe that just a half century ago, *damn* and *hell* were about as far anyone would go, and you had to stub your bare toe on a chair in the middle of the night to get away with those. So the Ex-Lax factory was a joke that we could share without someone telling our mothers and then being kept inside for a day to learn our lesson.

21

But the ice cream factory was even better than pretending a wall was covered in poop. Early in the morning we would hear the bells ringing on the trucks around the factory, which sounded like what the front of a Christmas card with a horse and a sleigh on it would sound like, if it had a sound.

"Hey Vinnie, you going to the ice cream factory?" Jimmy asked.

"Yeah, I think I might," said Vinnie, who walked funny because his right foot was turned in so far he looked like a clown. No one ever asked about his foot and he never said anything. He just walked funny. No one laughed at him.

And of course he was going to the ice cream factory. What a stupid question. Every kid in the neighbourhood headed for the ice cream factory every morning of every summer. The bells were calling us.

Once we turned the corner we could see the row of white Chevy pickup trucks parked with their backs against the curb. More trucks were waiting to get in. And while they waited, the drivers tested their bells because the bells paid their rent and bought them food. The bells made saliva flow and sent the kids running into their homes to yell, "Momma, Momma, ice cream man!" The bells were the advanced marketing team for the mobile ice cream industry.

Nowadays, ice cream trucks have sound systems that play a song that has nothing to do with ice cream and does not shut off when the truck stops. It is so annoying that mothers run out of their houses waving their fists at the ice cream trucks, shouting, "Shut up, shut up, you are waking the baby and I'll have my husband who is a lawyer sue you."

Back then, the bells on the Bungalow Bar trucks were tinkling and friendly. The driver pulled a bell cord with his right hand and steered with his left, and the bells on the roofs of the trucks put music on the side streets.

When the drivers shifted gears, the bells stopped. When they scratched their noses, the bells stopped. When they got out to sell Popsicles to kids on the curb, the bells stopped.

"We'll test your bells for you," we said as we walked between the trucks.

"We'll wash your truck," we said, holding a rag and an empty coffee can full of water.

We washed and tested and then stood by the back of the truck. We could go swimming later, but early in the morning we were hoping for something else. "Got any free ice cream?"

We almost never got any. These guys were working for a profit of a nickel on a pop. They were not going to give anything away when they could count their survival on Popsicle sticks. The only free stuff we got was the occasional broken pop or something that was stillborn in the freezer with the paper wrapping buried inside the ice cream.

The company was named Bungalow Bar because the icebox on the back of each truck was made to look like a summer bungalow, with shingles on the sides and a sloping roof on top. It was a country dream home in an area where no one had ever seen a house with a pointed roof. In fact, no one had actually seen a single-family house. All of our living spaces were covered with flat black tar, which was a beach in the summer and a safe playground for most of the year, provided you didn't chase a ball too fast or too far.

The ice cream was kept cold with dry ice, or "hot ice," as we called it.

"Hey, Tommy, look, I'm smoking." Vinnie would slip a piece of hot ice in his mouth and blow smoke through his lips. He had to keep the ice moving around over a wet tongue or it would burn a hole in his flesh. But all of us could do the smoke-from-the-lips trick. There were always slivers of broken ice on the street after the trucks loaded up. We played who could hold it in their hands the longest and who could hold it between their teeth.

But one glorious day a whole box of dry ice broke open on the street and the company left it there. It was steaming and evaporating in the hot sun when we spotted it. A pack of kids will descend on anything that looks different, especially when it looks like it will annoy others. Vinnie picked up a chunk that must have weighed five pounds. He needed both hands and dropped it a second later because it was burning his fingers. Others tried to pick up big pieces but quickly started jumping and hollering because that much dry ice hurts bare skin.

"I have an idea," said Buster. "If we put a piece in water you know what happens, right?"

We nodded. Buster was small but smart.

"Suppose we . . ." and he pointed to a sewer.

We had twenty pounds of dry ice. In ten minutes there were kids at every one of the five sewers on the street. Below us lay an ocean of stagnant city water and we were an army of kiddie saboteurs waiting for a string of factory delivery trucks.

They came in bunches, and when they came, mothers

with baby carriages could not cross the street. No one could play stickball. Even the rats weren't safe.

Five minutes later we heard a truck turning the corner. There would be more trucks behind it. "Now," shouted Tommy. He waved his arms and other kids up and down the block waved their arms, and large hunks of dry ice went down through five steel gratings.

Burp. Boil. Poof, a bubble of white steamy smoke rose back up through a grating. In a minute, white smoke began creeping up over all the steel sewer plates and began spreading out over the street. In two minutes, it was six inches deep and you couldn't see your feet. This was before Disneyland opened and before everyone had heard the term *special effects*. This was a street changing into a fantasyland. Windows opened. People came out and stood on their front steps. And the delivery trucks slowed to a creeping roll. No one even honked their horns. The drivers had never seen this before. If we were being invaded by aliens, this was the first wave.

"It's beautiful," said Vinnie. He had never said anything in his life was beautiful before that.

For fifteen minutes our street was quiet. It was no longer a factory area with drudgery as its main product. It was a setting now for a prince and princess. Dorothy and Vanessa came out of their houses. They were girls we were all in love with, and they danced through the strange white mist and picked up handfuls of it and threw it in the air.

It was the first, and last, time we ever heard the old ladies who were looking out their windows say "Oooh" and "Aaah."

And then it went away, and the trucks started up and the people went back inside.

I sit in movie houses now and watch special effects that invent entire universes. Bah, they know nothing. Pictures on a screen are only good for looking at. We created real special effects. We changed reality. We turned a dull street into a fantasyland, and those who were there still talk about it.

Sex and Basketball

Before Vanessa became one of our friends, she was the new girl whose family moved in at the end of the street, just under the elevated train line. She was from somewhere in South America. We didn't know where South America was, but we did fall in love with Vanessa. She was in grade seven. Her older sister was in high school and we never got to know her name. But when we were eleven and twelve, we all were having fantasies about Vanessa with the large chest.

She had dark hair and a pretty face, and most of all she had breasts. They were really there under her shirt. You could even see them under her coat. When she walked by we stopped breathing. Sometimes she smiled at us and we knew that she knew that we were looking at her, and this knowledge opened all the chemical faucets inside boys whose faces were just starting to grow pimples.

The back of her apartment and her bedroom window were just across a lane from the ice cream factory. She lived on the second floor and the factory was two storeys high. Eventually we figured out that if we climbed up on the roof of the factory and timed it right, we could watch Vanessa undress. Or at least we thought we could.

"Does she really?" asked Vinnie.

"Every night at ten," said Tommy, who lived nearby and knew what time the light came on.

"Ten's pretty late to be out," said Johnny.

"You could see her naked," said Bobby.

Silence. We thought about Vanessa without clothes.

"I'll see you tonight," said Vinnie.

"Me too," I said, with visions of uncovered and unknown skin dancing in my head.

We broke up and went home because it was getting dark and it was suppertime, and if any of us were late we would be in deep trouble, and if we got into trouble we would not be allowed out. Can you imagine being kept in the house, locked in and told no way are you leaving and you are going to wash the dishes and then do your home-work, and then having to go to bed, and while your friends are watching Vanessa undress, you are staring at the ceiling?

So we went home on time and we were as polite as could be. "Yes, ma'am, I would like some spinach." "No, thank you, I don't care for any more bread."

"What's the matter?" said Tommy's father. "I think you did something wrong."

"No sir, not me," said Tommy. "I didn't do nothing wrong, not me, no sir," he said, while thinking of Vanessa naked and worried that if he looked guilty his father would find some reason to keep him in. "On second thought, I don't want any spinach."

At nine o'clock, half a dozen boys told their parents that they were going out to play basketball.

"The schoolyard's locked," said Bobby's mother.

"We're going to play at the end of the street," said Bobby.

"There's no place to play at the end of the street," said Bobby's father.

"We're going to make a basketball hoop," said Bobby.

"It's dark," said Bobby's mother.

"We're just going to plan it," said Bobby.

At nine-fifteen, half a dozen boys were squeezing their way between the cold cinderblock garages behind Vanessa's apartment.

"Sssshhh. If they hear us they'll call the cops."

At nine-twenty, in the dark and with the cold autumn air working through our thin jackets, half a dozen boys were climbing onto a garage roof and then making a flying leap across two arm-lengths of space to the roof of the factory. At nine twenty-five we lay side by side on the tar roof with our heads propped up on our hands, staring at the back of a dark apartment window.

"I bet she's beautiful with no clothes on," said Tommy.

"I once saw a naked girl, but she was my cousin," said Vinnie.

"That doesn't count," I said.

We lay there for ten minutes before Tommy said, "I'm so cold I can't feel my thing any more."

"You will when she shows up," said Vinnie.

"Suppose we get caught," said Johnny. "They could arrest us as peeping toms."

"We'll just say we lost a ball on the roof," said Tommy.

"So why are we trying to find it at night?" asked Johnny.

"Because I got it for my birthday and if we don't find it we'll be in trouble," said Tommy.

Ten more minutes and we were clenching our teeth to keep them from chattering.

"If she doesn't come soon I'm going to have to go home," said Vinnie.

We all had the same problem, but Tommy said, "For this, getting in trouble will be worth it."

It was ten after ten. We knew the time because the Sealtest Milk Company had a big billboard on the other side of the railroad tracks that said Any Time Is the Right Time for Milk, and it had a clock. Hence, none of us ever got a watch for our birthdays or Christmas. The light came on in the window and we went rigid. We could see right into the bedroom. It was going to happen. Vanessa walked in and started combing her hair. We gasped. She began braiding her hair. We crawled closer to the edge of the roof.

"Can you see that?"

"Look at that!"

"Holy cow!"

This was all said in whispers while she finishing doing her hair.

Then, in answer to all our hopes and wishes and dreams and secret prayers, Vanessa started to unbutton her shirt.

"Oh, God." It was a gasp. It was going to happen.

She took off her shirt and we saw a white bra for almost a full second before her sister walked into the room and went to the window and pulled down the shade.

30

"She knows we are here," said Tommy, who was trying to stand up while keeping his head hidden.

"No way, she can't," said Vinnie.

But we knew we had been spotted. Why else would she have pulled the shade so fast and so firmly? We fell over each other trying to get off the roof before we were caught. We jumped to the garage roof and then down to the ground. There must be a god who cleaned away the broken bottles and cinder blocks and garbage cans from our landing pad because we didn't look before we leaped, but we didn't get hurt. We hit the ground and just kept running.

"Did you see her?" shouted Bobby as he ran. "I mean, did you see her bra?"

"She was almost naked," Vinnie said, while the night air blew past his face and his feet pounded down the sidewalk toward the end of our street.

When we stopped running we fell over each other laughing and talking and describing how much nakedness we had seen.

"I swear she almost had her bra off. I swear I saw it," said Jimmy Lee.

"I saw her naked. I mean I saw it, just before the shade went down. Didn't you see her?" That was Bobby, who sat on the curb with a smile and a faraway look.

We all went home that night with an excitement in our bodies that we had not known before. It was blissful.

"How'd the basketball game go?" Tommy's father asked.

Blankness. Followed by blood draining from Tommy's face. When his father looked down, he would know exactly what had happened.

"Fine, really fine," Tommy said.

"Maybe tomorrow night I'll come down and see what you accomplished," said his father.

"No, not tomorrow," said Tommy. "I mean, we're not done yet."

The next morning Tommy and Vinnie and Johnny and Bobby and I gathered at the end of the block and tried to find some way of turning the street into a basketball court. We had the ball, which we had stolen from the school, but no way to play with it because as Bobby's mother had said, the schoolyard, which had baskets, was locked at night.

"My father doesn't believe me," said Tommy.

"How do we make a basket?" asked Vinnie.

"Don't know," said Tommy.

But Johnny, who would grow up to be a home renovator, was picking through some pallets that were piled alongside a factory wall. Johnny's father had never taught his son anything about tools. He was always in the bar on the corner of the street. But somehow Johnny had learned how to build things on his own and he could take apart discarded pallets and make forts out of them that were strong enough for a bunch of kids to stand on top of. Inside the forts he could escape from whatever it was that happened to him at home when his father left the bar.

In an hour Johnny had a pallet ripped apart and hammered back together with a two-by-four backing and we had a backboard that weighed twenty-five pounds and wouldn't crack if a truck drove over it.

More kids came out on the street. Some went off to get a rope and others to find bigger nails around the factories.

Most of them were bent but we could straighten them. And Johnny got on Vinnie's back next to a telephone pole and Vinnie boosted him up so that he could grab onto the spikes that were used by the linemen to climb the poles.

Johnny on the pole was an event. A bunch of kids doing something was an event.

"Hey Johnny," Mr. Bellmeyer shouted from his window. "You finally get a job or are you playing Tarzan?"

"You be careful, Johnny," said Mrs. Zuppini, whose husband had died a year ago and so she wore all black and still had a black ribbon on her front door.

When Johnny had got about ten feet up, we threw the rope to him and he slung it over a spike and dropped one of the ends down. We tied the backboard onto it and then a bunch of guys pulled, and the board swung out over the street, then swung back and crashed into the pole. But with four guys holding the rope, Johnny got the board straightened and nailed into the pole and he climbed down. We had a backboard.

"Where's the hoop?" asked Buster, proving once again that he was smarter than the rest of us.

And I know it may sound contrived and unbelievable, but the only hoop we could come up with was made of three wire coat hangers that we straightened and twisted together and made into a circle big enough for the ball to go through. Johnny climbed the pole again and nailed the coat hanger hoop onto the board and the game began, lit by the street light twenty feet farther up the pole.

Vanessa was there, and Dorothy and Eileen and all the boys. We chose up sides and even Buster, who was only half as tall as Tommy, got to play. Joey's mother brought out Junior, Joey's brother, who had cerebral palsy and who could only walk in lurches and who couldn't speak, and the two of them leaned against a parked car and watched.

"Let Junior play," said Vanessa, and she took his hand and led him out onto the street while he drooled and shrieked. Someone held the ball up for him, but he only flailed with his arms and smacked it away.

Then Vinnie threw the ball at the basket and it hit the wire and bent it in. And Tommy made the next shot and the wire bent some more.

"Good shot," said Tommy's father who had come out and was watching from across the street.

Tommy grabbed the ball from another kid and drove across the street, dribbling around a sewer plate and even putting it between his legs, not daring to look back in case his father was no longer there. He shot and turned his head. His father was watching. The ball hit the hoop and bent it some more.

"Not bad," said his father.

The game went on for fifteen minutes, stopping occasionally for cars, although at night when the factories were closed, the traffic was so light it was hardly a challenge.

"This is great." "This is wonderful." "This is the best game ever." Who said that? It doesn't matter. We all said it, even though no one was quite sure who was on each side, and the score was still nothing–nothing, because the hoop was so flattened the ball could not get through it.

When we quit we were laughing and Junior was running in circles and jumping and Mrs. Zuppini was clapping.

"Time to come in," said Buster's mother.

Dorothy and Vanessa said goodnight to each other and we watched Vanessa walk up the street, but tonight it would be more fun to sit on the curb and talk about the game. Besides, we were tired.

Eventually we all headed home, including Johnny, who stopped for a minute to watch his father stagger out of the bar.

The next day we talked about basketball, but we went back to playing stickball. A broom handle and a rubber ball were easier to get than another hoop. Throughout the fall and winter our games changed from street-level baseball to football, all played under the street light and under the backboard and crumpled hoop. And although we talked basketball, we never played again.

In time we moved away. Vanessa got a religious calling in her sixteenth year and became a nun. Johnny moved to Florida and made so much money building houses that he started building them for poor people. Joey got married and moved away and his parents got old and had to put Junior in a home. One day Joey went to visit Junior and found him tied up, with his hands behind his back. He took him home and cared for him and took him out to watch professional basketball games, much to the distress of those who sat next to him.

Forty years later I returned to that street. It was quieter. The elevated train at the end of the block had been cut down. The ice cream factory was closed and the new factory in the same building was making razor wire. The bar at the end of the street had its windows all covered over with brick. The factory at the end of the street was deserted.

As I walked down my old street I heard only Spanish. Little kids played in front of their homes with their mothers watching. Teenagers watched me. I was a stranger. Neighbourhoods are sacred places and intruders are carefully watched. Halfway down the block I stopped at a telephone pole. About ten feet up, nailed to the pole was one small shred of wood, no bigger than an outstretched hand. You had to hunt to see it. No hoop, no backboard, just one piece of wood with a nail in it.

I blinked my eyes, and suddenly Vanessa and Dorothy and Tommy and Johnny and Joey and Junior and Vinnie were there on the street. And a ball was thrown at the hoop and it bent the hoop. Kids were running around the street, and I could feel the sweat on my head as I tried to shoot for the wire and missed.

When the ball landed, there were kids watching me, whispering in Spanish. They didn't see the game. They saw an odd man staring up at a telephone pole. They didn't see the greatest basketball ball game ever played. They didn't see the kids who were a chapter in the history of their street. They didn't see the backboard. And most of all, they didn't see the personal heaven that appeared just as the clouds in my eyes parted.

The Asphalt Gridiron

Forget the bets on who is going to win the next Super Bowl. I'll lay you ten to one, cold cash, right now, that no matter what the score is, most folks will say, "The bums were boring. Midget football has more soul."

Big games are usually like that—lots of hype followed by a linebacker-sized letdown. I will tell you how I know this: I was on the field in a game bigger than the Super Bowl. It was a time when we actually played football instead of watching it on television.

It was in the autumn and winter, when the sun set early and it was too dark to see a small rubber ball even under the street light, that we had to give up our beloved baseball. But a football was big enough to see even when it came out of the black sky, so we could choose up sides and play with the cold air in our faces until we were exhausted. Girls played, boys played, but because the field was a hard asphalt street, we didn't have tackling. We had to touch the ball carrier with two hands to stop the play.

"You didn't get me with both hands." "Did so!" "Didn't!" "Did!" "Didn't!" And so on, until someone grabbed the ball and went on with the game. The seasons and years passed by under our feet while we jumped out of the way of cars and dodged the voices of mothers yelling for us to come in and do homework.

And then we all reached the ages of eleven and twelve and thirteen at about the same time, including the girls. And it became football season again—touch football. So when we chose up sides, it was really important to get some girls on each side because we couldn't actually date these girls. After all, they were our friends, and none of us knew anything about dating anyway. But we had this—well, urge to run after them and, if we were lucky, to touch them.

The girls were different. They tried hard not to get touched. This was a very basic Catholic/Jewish/Protestant neighbourhood where all the girls were taught to avoid boys except in church, in school and on their wedding night. But the boys talked about touching, dreamed about touching and made up lies about touching. And so we lived for football.

Then, one night when we did not expect it, came our Super Bowl. For reasons no one could ever figure out, or ever tried to, all the girls wound up on one side. We boys got into a huddle, and with our butts sticking up and our heads down, we looked at each other in joyous disbelief. This was going to be the luckiest night of our lives.

There was just one thing we didn't know: the girls had been practising.

We kicked off and they received, and just as Tommy's hands were about to make contact with Dorothy, who was carrying the ball, she threw a lateral pass to Eileen, which meant that Dorothy couldn't be touched.

"Where did you learn that?" asked Tommy.

Dorothy just sniggered and ran off.

Then Eileen did the same thing just before Johnny tagged her. A lateral pass is when you throw the ball sideways or backward, and it only works if you know that someone is there to catch the ball. It is very good football. And they did it again and again. Then they got a touchdown.

A team of frustrated boys got into a huddle again. The heck with touching them, someone said, let's just stop them. But the game got worse. One of the girls went back for a long pass and she caught the ball on the other side of the fire hydrant. Touchdown. Again.

Finally we got the ball, but they intercepted it before we were two car-lengths down the street. They outpassed us, they outran us, but most of all they avoided us—and our hands.

They beat us twenty-one or thirty-one or maybe it was forty-one to nothing. The score would have been worse except that a couple of the boys on our team thought they heard their mothers calling them. "Sorry, guys, I got to go do my homework."

Real Super Bowls are like that. Big hype, but empty hands.

THE STAKEOUT

W hen I retire, I am going to be a cowboy. It's a career suggested to me by a patient man a long time ago, after I finished my work in law enforcement. That lasted only a short time, but I can still say on my resumé that I was a cop with my own beat, which I single-handedly cleaned up. My name was Officer Mike, and my job was to fight crime and protect the innocent. That is what my Uncle John told me when he swore me in.

My Uncle John was a cop, a tough New York City cop with a badge and a gun. He had worked the streets for years, and by the time I got to know him he had been promoted and he worked as a detective in the homicide squad. I worshipped my uncle, which is not an unusual thing to do when you are six.

He shared his home with my mother and father and me because he lived alone and my father was often drunk and my mother had nowhere else to go. My father and uncle were brothers, but they were not the same kind of person. My uncle also brought me little toys whenever he came back from his trips, even if he only got the toy from the corner store before walking into the house. And he was always happy and fun to be with. My father, on the other hand, spent most of his days in the bar and then staggered back home, and my mother told me that one of the first games I played was fall down drunk like Daddy. Hence, I liked my uncle a lot more than my father.

I would be waiting for him when he came home from work in the morning. He would usually bring along some policemen friends of his and they would sit at the kitchen table while my mother cooked them breakfast. I sat under the table and looked at their guns. All policemen in New York carry several pistols, and most strap one to their legs. Policemen there are also required to be armed even when they are off-duty and having breakfast. So I would sit under the table and listen to them laugh and talk about chasing the bad guys. That was the kind of life I wanted.

"Uncle John, can I be a junior policeman?" I would ask.

"Well, you are not quite old enough," he would say, and then he would chase me around the house until I hid behind the couch.

"Bang, bang," I would say.

"Oh, you got me," he would say. "I have to go to bed and get better."

After dinner, when he had woken up and had his breakfast, I would ask again. "Can I be a policeman now?"

"Not until you are older."

"Can I be a policeman tomorrow, then?"

"Maybe tomorrow, but make sure you keep your mother safe tonight," he would say.

Then he got dressed for work. He no longer wore a uniform, just a suit. But he didn't get ready like other men going to work. He put a blackjack into his back pocket and hooked handcuffs over his belt. Then he checked the bullets in one gun and slipped it into the holster under his arm. And then he checked his other gun and pulled up his pants leg and slid the gun into the holster on his leg. I sat on his bed every night and watched and said, "I want to be like you, Uncle John."

Then he went to work, after telling my mother that if his brother got violent she should lock herself and me in the bedroom. At times when she did this, she told me not to worry because Daddy would never break down the door in Uncle John's house because he knew Uncle John would be very mad and Daddy was afraid of Uncle John. Some nights we lay in bed while the pounding on the door got weaker and weaker and then stopped. And the next morning Uncle John would come back and everything would be fine again.

"Hello, Uncle John. Can I be a policeman now?"

When I think back now, I remember that not all mornings were happy meals with friends gathered around fried eggs and the smell of coffee in the air. Some mornings, like this one, he had band-aids on his hands and his tie was pulled down and he was alone and tired.

"Can I?"

He took off his hat and rubbed my head.

"OK, I think the time has come," he said.

"What! Really? Now?!" I jumped. I hugged him. I ran to my mother. "I'm going to be a policeman." I ran back to him. "Really?"

"Yes, really," he said.

We stepped into his bedroom, which was next to the kitchen, and he took a card out of his dresser drawer. It was the top drawer where he kept his bullets. I knew this because I had climbed up there several times and opened it and looked inside, but I never touched any of the bullets because he had once told me that if I ever dropped one it would blow up the whole house, which had four families living in it. So I just looked, then quietly closed the drawer and sneaked away.

The card he was holding said New York City Police Dept., and it had a police badge printed on it and his name. I couldn't read very well, but I recognized the badge. It looked like my uncle's badge. And on the back of the card he wrote something. I couldn't read that either, except for my name. He said it made me a junior policeman.

Then he told me to raise my hand and swear that I would uphold the law and be good to people. I promised.

"But what about catching crooks?" I asked.

"If you see any, you tell me. But first you protect your mother."

He went to bed and I strapped on my plastic six-shooter, put the card with the badge on it in my shirt pocket, and asked my mother if I could go outside.

Standing on the sidewalk I pulled up the card so that the part with the badge could be seen. That is when I saw Mrs. Gaggle, who lived next door, blow her nose in a tissue and then throw the tissue toward the street. It landed on the sidewalk and she ignored it. I held up my card and talked to her. A short time later I saw Mr.

David take a newspaper from his neighbour's front steps. I spoke to him too.

I marched up and down the sidewalk, walking my beat, checking the alley and picking up some litter. Two or three times I pulled the card from my pocket and looked at the badge. I was going to be the best cop this town ever saw. Then I saw that goofy neighbour kid Herbert. He was a teenager and he had tattoos on his knuckles that said "love" and "hate." He showed them to everyone. He also smoked, and he didn't go to school and he didn't go to work. He was going to be a criminal, I knew. But today he was walking his big, ugly dog, which had a heavy chain around its neck, and he let the dog poop on the sidewalk, right in the middle of where people walk. That was illegal, and yucky. I touched the handle of my pistol as I walked up to him.

The next morning I couldn't wait for Uncle John to come home. When he walked in the door with friends, I knew it was a good morning. Then I told him about all the crimes I had seen. His friends were laughing and telling him what a good job he had done in training me.

Then I told him I had arrested all these criminals.

"What do you mean 'arrested'?"

"I told them they had to come and see you this morning," I said, "and that you would take them to jail."

That is when my uncle sat me up on his knee, and with his shoulder holster near my face, he suggested that maybe I should be a cowboy instead of a policeman. Then I could teach him how to be a cowboy because that is what he secretly, honestly wanted to be.

So when I finish this current career, I am going to saddle up a horse. My Uncle John, with his blackjack and guns, was patient and kind when he could have gotten angry. The least I can do is take his memory for a peaceful ride across the countryside.

Later, when I became a reporter, I worked for a newspaper that had a great library. You could look up almost anything about any place or any situation or any person. There were reporters who had contacts at the CIA and the FBI and who knew backroom politicians, and the information they obtained was stored in the library. I looked up my name. And there, under the same last name, was my uncle. There were pictures of him taken by undercover police as he collected payoffs from illegal gambling and booze joints. He resigned before he was prosecuted. He was crooked. He was my uncle whom I loved more than any adult male in my life. He was like many of us, very good and very bad.

I am still going to take that horseback ride.

Laundry Room Lessons

You know that book that was a million best-seller a few years ago, *All I Really Need To Know I Learned In Kindergarten?*

Well, I have the comic book version, the twenty-five-cent equivalent: *Everything I Learned About Living I Learned in the Laundry Room.*

For a while we lived in an apartment building, and all the women brought their dirty shirts and underwear down to the basement, which was a dank and humid place with rows of rusting washing machines. The women brought their kids along because there was nowhere else to leave them. And it was while I sat on top of white porcelain-and-metal boxes with water sloshing below my bottom that I heard the news. Old man Jenkins was drinking again, and Mr. Rupert was talking to that hussy in 6D while she was sunbathing on the roof.

These were hard-working women who talked about plain life. They did not exchange information on how to get their clothes whiter than white. That is a silly fable made up by advertising companies. What they were interested in were the people in the apartment house, and how they were doing in the journey through existence. They had the best stories, better than radio or TV soap operas, and better than the movies. These stories were real, and I knew the characters.

Sometimes I got to watch an actual drama unfold when the women were talking about someone and she walked into the room. "Oh! Hello, dearie. Oh, noooo! That wasn't you we were talking about. Oh, heavens no. That was someone whose name *sounds* just like yours. She's a witch. Not you." I sat on a machine and watched faces turn red and hands get busy folding clothes.

But mostly I heard stories that were so gripping I forgot to blink. Stories that scared me, like the man beating his wife and children. And stories that made me laugh, like the woman who ran out of hairspray and used varnish instead.

They were stories that made the world go around: who was pregnant, who was having an affair, who had gotten fired and who had won big at the track. They were stories you could repeat for days and everyone who heard them wanted to hear more.

Every story had a moral to it, and from these wise women I learned some of life's more practical lessons. These are the ten commandments handed up from the laundry room. The first five are cautions:

1. If you are mean, people won't like you and they will wish bad things for you.
2. If you fool around with the hussy in 6D, you will be the only one who thinks it is a secret.
3. If you spend more time watching TV than playing with your kids, your kids will forget you.

4. If you lose at gambling, you will be laughed at. If you win, others will be jealous and want to borrow money. So, don't gamble.
5. If something bad happens to you, people will feel sorry for you. If you feel sorry for yourself, people will avoid you.

The next five are more positive bywords:

6. Feeding birds is almost as good as going to church.
7. If you smile when you say hello, people will be glad you are alive.
8. If you hold a door for the next person, you will be a hero in their eyes.
9. If you spend time listening to old people, you will be a saint.

And most important:

10. If you lend someone soap powder for the washing machine, you will have a place in heaven.

No one who has followed these rules has ever done badly in life. It is a pity so many people have washing machines at home now. It cheats kids out of great stories, and even greater wisdom.

Truck Watching

You probably know that birdwatching is one of the most popular hobbies in the Western world. What you may not know is that one of the best birdwatchers on the planet came from my old neighbourhood, which didn't have any birds to speak of except sparrows and pigeons.

I'll tell you more about Billy the birder in a minute. But first, a word about this pastime whose popularity seems to be related to age. The older the population, the more people there are creeping through parks looking for little things in trees. And it is not just binoculars that they carry, but notebooks, palm pilots and tape recorders to whisper into, because birdwatching is no longer simply enjoyable. It is now a competitive sport.

There are birders who have lists a thousand names long. Now it is the humans, not the birds, who fly across the country at the report of a new sighting. They watch the Internet more closely than the sky, because on the World Wide Web there are reports of birds that have gone astray during migration and that translates into one more potential name to collect.

49

Now, back to the little brown sparrows and Billy and our neighbourhood. We had heard about birdwatching, but we never understood why people would go out of their way to look at something that you could see any old time, just by throwing some bread crumbs on the street. But most of all we did not care about spotting birds because we had something better. We had a highway that went through a sunken cut a block from our street, and unlike birds, the creatures on that highway came to us. They had noise and size and speed and they were the kings of the road. They were trucks. Big trucks.

We would sit on a railing above the cut and watch them roar by down below while they blew their diesel smoke up in our faces and sometimes their horns in our ears.

But you know you can't be satisfied with just watching. We turned it into a game. We taught ourselves to pick out a Kenworth at a quarter mile just by the shape of the cab. A line of dirty-faced boys and girls balanced on the railing, and when a truck was barely visible, someone would shout, "Looks like a Mack."

"No, you idiot. That's an International."

As it got closer and we could see the shape better, someone would say, "White. It's a White." And in five seconds a White tractor pulling a trailer would barrel by below us, blowing our hair around and throwing dirt into our faces. The one who got it right was cheered and elbowed in the ribs by the others, and for a moment he or she was the pick of the litter. You feel good when your friends praise you.

And we deserved the praise. You had to be quick, since most of us could spot the difference between a Freightliner and Western Star without hesitation. It was just a case of appreciating what was real in our world.

Now, back to Billy. He was an observational grand master. He could tell the make of the truck by the sound of the motor. We held our hands over his eyes and he would say, "Sounds like a Mack with a full trailer."

We looked down and saw a Mack, straining up an incline with a full trailer.

"How'd you do that?" we asked.

"Concentration," said Billy. He would sit for hours watching trucks and memorizing the sounds they made.

Then we grew up and left the highway behind and I lost track of Billy. But one day, years later, I read in the newspaper about a champion birdwatcher. He had won a big, lucrative contest by spotting the most birds on a list in one day in one park.

It was Billy. The story said he was out in the field with the other contestants, but he barely looked up. He just kept scribbling names down on his list. He got ten birds while the others were hunting through the branches for one. The story went on to say that Billy was one of the strangest birdwatchers ever to enter the contest. It said that he had learned his skill as a child, but would not tell his secret. He would only say: "Compared to a Kenworth, a robin just whispers its name. And it doesn't blow smoke in your face."

GHOST FIGHTERS

You know that time just after the sun has set and before you get called in for dinner, in the winter, when it gets dark early and you have an hour or two to feel grown up by being out late.

That is when we went out on manoeuvres to protect the country. In fact we were safeguarding the whole Western world. We were soldiers and we were ready for the enemy. Most of us were ten or eleven years old and we had broomsticks for rifles. You may have served in that same army once, fighting foes on a different front.

Our commander-in-chief was John Wayne. He taught us to be brave and never to fear anyone. We had seen him in the movies leading charges against whole battalions without even buckling his helmet strap.

The enemy always attacked at night, when our fingers were cold and we were low on ammunition. If the battle was on our own street, the attacks were easy to beat back.

"Pow, pow, bang. I got him."

Rifle fire filled our voices, but it was mostly from our side because the enemy couldn't find us. We knew the street well and we had all the hiding places memorized. There was safety behind the front stairs and under the parked cars.

Then one day one of us said that the next battle was going to be hard. The enemy was taking over the cemetery and we would have to liberate it. The cemetery was almost ten blocks away and some of us might be late for dinner, but it was the price we had to pay to be like John Wayne.

We started off just as the streets were getting dark, and we carried our weapons on our shoulders because we didn't want anyone thinking they were only broomsticks. Folks may smirk at kids, but no one laughs at a soldier. By the time we got to the cemetery, it was dark and we could hardly see the fence around it. It was a tall chain-link fence, and that was the first time we stopped, not because of the fence but because of Buster.

"You believe in ghosts?" he asked.

In our zeal to protect the world, we had not considered the other world.

"Come on, " said Tommy. "There are no such things as ghosts."

But Buster was not climbing the fence, and Vinnie said, "Maybe we shouldn't go in there."

Vinnie had no doubt about ghosts because his mother had seen one when she was a little girl, and therefore the family had never missed a Sunday in church, and if he or anyone in his family ever made the mistake of pointing at a graveyard, they had to bite their finger or they would have bad luck. There are things that you do not take lightly.

"Maybe we shouldn't go in there," Vinnie said again.

"Don't be a chicken," said Tommy. "You think John Wayne would be afraid?"

John Wayne, the hero of cowboy movies and war

movies, who always stood up to the bad guy, would not be afraid of ghosts. We wanted to be heroes so we all climbed the fence, even Buster and Vinnie.

The ground on the other side was different. It was not like being on the outside. This was a whole unmapped battlefield, with statues of angels and silhouettes of tombs against the sky. There were no lights. We could see the city on the other side of the darkness, but we were inside, locked inside, trapped inside.

"Ouch." Buster had stubbed his foot on something that didn't move. He reached down, touched something, then shrieked.

"Shut up," said Tommy.

"It's a gravestone," said Buster. "I kicked a gravestone. That's against the law, isn't it?"

"What about the war?" said Tommy.

"I don't want to play any more," said Buster.

"Soldiers can't be afraid," said Tommy. He moved ahead and we followed.

There was a little gunfire, but the bullets coming from our weapons were much quieter than they had ever been on our street. Amid a few pops and pows, we advanced.

"I think we . . ." It was Vinnie's voice, but he didn't finish. Just silence. He dropped his broomstick. "Oh, God, look at that."

Tommy froze. Buster started shaking. Vinnie backed away. In front of us were two white forms, moving between the headstones. I am not making this up to be dramatic. As I sit here writing almost fifty years after that night, I can still remember my tongue sticking to the roof of my mouth and my knees quaking as the two white shapes glided very slowly through the night. They were barely visible, but we could see them well enough to terrified. Then one of them began to change shape and to grow larger and started coming toward us. Oh my gosh. Five little soldiers tried desperately not to cry.

We backed up slowly, then faster and faster until we were almost running backwards. Then we turned and dropped our rifles and ran past the headstones and hit the fence as high as we could jump. We didn't worry about the sharp ends of the twisted wires at the top. We were up and over it and we fell to the ground on the other side and ran, and we did not stop running until we were back on our own street.

We didn't worry about being like John Wayne. We didn't worry about getting home late. We didn't worry about whatever punishment we would get. We were so happy to be back under the noisy elevated train and near the bar with the jukebox and the drunks inside that we sat on the sidewalk talking and laughing in excitement, because we had a secret that we knew was true but we couldn't tell anyone because no one would believe us.

"I don't know what it was, but I'm never going back there," said Tommy.

"I should tell my mother," said Vinnie.

"Are you crazy?" we said. "She'd kill you for being in there."

So Vinnie kept his secret about the ghosts from his mother who had seen one, and we all stayed away from the cemetery. After that night we all gave up soldiering. It was time to leave John Wayne in the movies and get back to baseball.

Ten years later, after I graduated from high school, I got a job and had to walk past the cemetery to get there. I passed it many times, and then one summer day when I was early for work, I walked in through the open gates of the burial ground. It was well kept with rows of crowded headstones, and in my mind I saw us on that night of battle, hiding behind some of the stones. I walked farther and just over a small rise I reached a pond. And on the pond swam two beautiful white swans. As I watched, one of them lifted its wings, very slowly as swans do, and stretched itself. Our ghosts.

I walked to the edge of the pond. "We weren't really afraid of you that night," I told the swans. "Me and the other kids, we were just pretending."

Showdown on the Asphalt

There is a toy that every kid used to have, and a few smart ones still do. You could do just about anything with it, especially things electronic toys can't do. It has been played with during wars because it is small enough to be carried in a pocket. It has survived depressions because it cost almost nothing. Yet even rich kids played with it. Even if you don't have any in your home, you know I am talking about marbles: beautiful, simple, round pieces of glass that take as much or as little skill as anyone can put into them.

We had marble games that lasted all day—in fact, some lasted all summer. But before I tell you about Judy, the greatest marble player who ever lived, here is a short history of marbles.

The Romans and Egyptians had marbles made out of bones and stones, and as near as historians can figure out, they played marbles in much the same way as we do now. Lots of other pastimes are descendants of marbles. Golf owes everything to marbles. So do billiards, ten-pin bowling, English lawn bowling and bocce. They are all the grandchildren of marbles, a game that is like curling without getting your feet cold.

Now, back to Judy. She was about twelve and she played the same way, no matter whether it was on concrete or dirt. She would pop her bubble gum, then with chalk or her finger draw a circle on the ground, then invite anyone—and she meant anyone—to get down on their knees and hunch over close to the line and compete in a winner-take-all contest.

The rules: two kids would each put one marble in the circle. Once it was in there you could not touch it. Then one at a time, the players would get down with one eye pinched tight and their fingers right up to the line and they would fire out a marble and try to knock the other one out of the ring. If they did, the marble was theirs. If they missed and their marble went outside the ring, their marble bag got lighter. The rules were so simple it was called no-rules.

"You playing no-rules?"

"Yeah."

"OK, I'll play with you."

But there was something about the way Judy could get her thumb into the crook of her index finger that let her fire marbles anywhere she wanted. That made her the most feared of all shooters. Her reputation spread beyond our neighbourhood, and one day a kid from another neighbourhood got off a bus with a cloth bag hanging from his fist and a mean look in his eye.

"Where's Judy?" is all he said. He had a couple of friends with him. They looked just as mean.

"She's at the end of the street," a bunch of kids told him.

It was high noon when he walked up to her.

"Wanna play?" he said.

"Sure," she answered.

58

Kids gathered to watch the showdown on the asphalt.

They were kneeling at the circle when the kid opened his bag and took out the biggest marble any of us had ever seen. Our neighbourhood didn't have stores that sold marbles that big. His did. It was twice the size of Judy's.

You did not have to go to university to know that a little marble cannot move a much larger marble, at least not far enough to knock it out of the ring.

"Usual no-rules?" he said.

Judy took a deep breath, felt around in her cloth bag and pulled out a handful of cat's eyes and clearies. She took a few practice shots off to the side, and you could tell by her sagging shoulders that she knew she could not move that giant marble.

"Well, go ahead," said the boy.

Judy popped one more bubble, then smiled. Out from between her lips came a wad of gum. She wrapped it around her marble and rolled it in the dirt and gravel next to a signpost.

"You can't do that," said the boy.

"Remember, no-rules," she replied.

And then she fired her pebble-studded musket ball with a rubber bumper, and it slammed into his oversized attempt at fame, and one giant marble from another neighbourhood wound up on the outside of the ring.

The boy knew what he was up against. He cut his losses, picked up his bag and, followed at a distance by his friends, walked away from the circle and got on the next bus.

A Wet Slap in the Face

In some North American cities, it is against the law now to have a clothesline in your own yard. Apparently the spectacle of someone else's underwear and towels flapping in the breeze is unsightly. This is idiotic. It is a pity. It is a step backwards in our social evolution.

For one thing, it goes dead against ecological common sense. The sun and the wind do a wonderful job of drying clothes. Without them you have to use electricity, which you have to pay for and which comes from rivers that have been dammed, which stops fish from having babies. Plus miles of high-tension wires have to be strung down mountainsides and over trees, making a ridiculous sight in the wilderness.

But the worst aspect of banning clotheslines is that we are sterilizing the world and taking away one of the best games of summer. It is called hit the sheet.

Imagine tearing across a backyard at full speed on a hot day and hitting a blowing sheet that is still wet. The moment you touch the cold cotton, the burning of the sun is gone. You have happy skin. The cloth slips over your face so lightly and deliciously, you run in a circle so that you can do it again. It is like surfing. You wait for the right breeze to lift the perfect sheet. No, not that one, too high. Not that, it's just a puff. But the next breath of wind rises up under the sheet like a ghost with its arms out and you start your run. Contact. It is not a crash. It is a slap that caresses, and from the moment of contact until you come out the other side you are in a world of cool.

Except for the time when Tommy was playing hit the sheet. I guess Mrs. Fiddler, who had hung the sheet on the line, did not use enough clothespins that day, because when Tommy plowed into it head first, it stayed with him and kept going right across the backyard, turning Tommy into a ghost and leaving the clothesline bare. This was really funny and we were all laughing our heads off, until Tommy tripped and fell in the only patch of mud in that yard.

By the time we got him unwrapped, the white sheet had lumps and streaks of brown all over it. To say we were terrified wasn't close to half the truth. Everyone was scared of Mrs. Fiddler. She never looked happy, she never said hello, and at Christmas she never left a six-pack of beer on top of her garbage for the garbage men. "I don't know how she can call herself a Christian," said Tommy's mother to her children.

"What are we going to do?" said Helen. Helen was Tommy's little sister and she was looking at her big brother, who was crying.

We couldn't run away. We knew she would catch us. But she must have gone out, because if she were home, she would be yelling at us already. "We can clean it," said Jimmy

Lee, who lived next door to Mrs. Fiddler and knew that his would be the first door she would be knocking on. Jimmy went home and came back with a metal bucket he had got from his basement. It had dirt and ashes in it, because it was used for putting out cigarettes or for a place to put the stuff that got swept up from the basement floor, or both. We dumped it out and turned on a hose and tried to wash out the bucket quickly before Mrs. Fiddler came back. Jimmy took his favourite red cowboy bandana out of his back pocket and started scrubbing the bucket. Just because Tommy had caused the problem didn't mean that it was his problem alone. At six and seven you stick together.

"Quick, get the sheet in there. Quick, get the water on it. Quick, get some soap."

Soap? Where do you get soap?

"I can get soap," said Helen, and she took off flying down the alley with a mission to save her brother.

"I hope she doesn't get caught," said Tommy. We knew that kids didn't steal soap unless there was a big problem.

We were still scrubbing the middle of the sheet, which we had stuffed into the bucket, while other kids were holding the edges off the ground, when Helen came back with both hands full of soap powder. We scrubbed, and spilled some of the soap into the pail, and scrubbed some more. We were soaked but the sheet was still dirty, so we scrubbed harder and used more soap and got more soaked. We worked in panic, and eventually, thanks to the deity that hangs around kids when they play and have troubles, that sheet actually got clean. We held it out like a rescue blanket and hosed it to get the soap out, and we got more soaked.

"We have a problem," said Jimmy. He was looking up at the clothesline. It was at least ten feet off the ground, attached to the top of the window, and we knew without measuring ourselves that we did not come up to the bottom of the windowsill. The tallest of us were four and a half feet high.

We tried throwing it, but you can't throw a soaking wet full-size bed sheet and expect it to go where you want, except back on the ground. So we washed it again. Then four of us got a ladder that was hanging on the side of a garage and leaned it against the side of the house. We climbed up, carrying the sheet like a fire hose, and threw it over the line. Jimmy, who was at the top of the ladder, held the sheet while he pushed the line out underneath it. The pulley turned and the sheet actually unfurled, almost like when it was first hung up, except it was draped over the line and there were no clothespins on it.

Ten minutes later Mrs. Fiddler opened her window. She looked at the sheet, then looked around the yard. Before she even touched it, she shouted, "You kids, you're going to get into trouble someday!" We were hiding in the shadows between the garages with our hearts beating faster than when we were scrubbing.

She pulled the sheet halfway in and examined it, looking perplexed. She apparently did not see any dirt because she pushed the sheet out again with new clothespins holding it. Then she shouted, "I know you did something, wherever you are! And someday I'm going to catch you." Then she slammed the window shut so hard we thought it would break.

We still weren't breathing. A few minutes later we sneaked away down the alley, soaked and scared and excited.

Now, think of a community where there are no clotheslines. We may all be spared the sight of underwear, but it is the kids who have been hung out to dry.

ONE-CENT JOSÉ

Forget lumber and technology and tourism—gambling is the fastest growing industry in this country, bar none, and the government seems addicted to it. But there is one type of gambler the government wishes would go away: the kind who can actually beat the casino and the track. And the best example of that is a kid we called One-Cent José. He lived in my neighbourhood and he was to gambling what Castro is to Cuba: someone in total control. I mention Cuba because his parents had slipped out of there when Castro took over, and they had nothing in their pockets when they left.

José first set foot on my old street with a single penny and no English. The English was not a problem. He just stood on the corner flipping the penny in the air and catching it and flipping it again.

"Hi, kid," we said to him. "You new around here?"

He answered in Spanish. He didn't understand us. We didn't understand him. Then he tossed the penny against a wall.

"You want to toss pennies?" we asked.

He answered again in Spanish. It didn't matter that we didn't understand each other. We knew we had a contest, and we knew he knew it. One of our guys tossed a penny. It landed half an inch from the wall. It wasn't great, but it was a good shot.

José moved his arm in a circle as if he were directing music. Then he flipped out his coin.

Wow: it bounced off our guy's penny and landed just a fingernail ahead of it. He said something else in Spanish, then picked up both pennies. Half an hour later he had won twenty-five cents and we knew each other's names.

José spent the summer in that neighbourhood, learning English and flipping a lot of pennies against a wall. That was our main form—no, it was our only form—of gambling after Abe the bookie who worked in the dry cleaner's was arrested.

José had a knack for getting his coins to land closest to the wall on almost every shot. Some people play golf well. He tossed pennies very well. But the odd thing about him was that he never played with more than one cent. If he lost that on the first toss, he just stayed out of the game. That is why we started calling him One-Cent. Even though he had more money at home, he never took more than one penny with him when he went out to gamble. That was his secret. He was the only gambler I ever knew who actually had discipline.

We did not laugh at him. We knew that he was poor and that he dealt with his poverty by never losing more than one penny. Then one day some bigger kids talked One-Cent into playing with them. They knew his reputation, so after everyone had thrown out a penny, they said there was a new rule: everyone had to toss two pennies.

José picked up his coin.

"You can't do that. You got to throw another one," they said.

"I don't have another penny," said José.

"Then you lose this one," they said.

He looked at his penny on the ground. Then looked at them. Then he walked away. I remember the bigger kids calling him chicken and laughing at him. A couple of us walked with him back to his front door. We felt sorry for him, but we also felt disappointed because we knew he could beat them, if only he would just try again.

He asked us to wait a minute. Then he came out with a sock that was stretched with the weight of something heavy in it. "I have twenty-two dollars in here," he said. He was proud. He held the sock like a trophy. It was all pennies. He told us that when it got to be twenty-five dollars, he would give it to his parents.

"If I lose two cents, I would be cheating my mother and father," he said.

José is the kind of person that those in charge of racetracks, lotteries and casinos can't stand. He knows when to quit. I have been leaving my money in those same places for forty years, and José is the only person I've ever seen who has actually walked away a winner.

You could say he had discipline. You could also say he did not have greed. But for sure you would say that his heart, not his talent, was in charge.

The Man Who Loved Worms

He might have been crazy. We weren't sure. But we sure learned a lot from Gus. He taught us how to hold a baseball bat and how to steal second base. He used to play in the minors, on a double-A ball team, which means that if he had made it to the triple-A team he would have been only one step below the majors.

Then he was hit in the head by a bad pitch, in the time before batters began to wear helmets. After that he just wandered around, unable to play and unable to hold a job for long. Sometimes he would get some work sweeping floors or unloading trucks, but he was never fast enough and he would eventually get fired.

"You do a hook slide by coming around," Gus was telling a bunch of us one afternoon. He sat on the front steps of the house he shared with his sister and his mother. His sister was the only one of them who went to work. She left at night and there was a rumour that she did things most of us could not imagine.

The guys in the bar always stood by the window that had Pat's Bar and Grill written on it and watched her as she walked past toward the subway. "You know where she's going," they would say with a smirk. We youngsters, who were sitting at the doorway of the bar so that we would feel grown up, would hear them and repeat, "You know where she's going."

Gus said she was a telephone operator.

"If you are going to do a hook slide, you have to bend your legs so you can steer yourself around the bag. But it can hurt."

We didn't care about Gus's sister and we didn't care what people said about him. We cared about hook slides—until it rained. That's when Gus did the thing that made him odd, and we could only watch and feel sorry for him.

"There he goes again," our parents would say. "Crazy, crazy Gus."

In a downpour he would walk the sidewalks picking up worms that were crawling on the concrete. He would squat, slip a fingernail under a worm, scoop it up and carry it gently in the palm of his hand to a patch of dirt and place the worm under a bush or under some leaves. People walking on the sidewalk, bent under their umbrellas, would leave a lot of space between themselves and Gus.

The worms came from the tiny patches of dirt in front of the houses. These patches had once been gardens, but now they were mostly just dirt with weeds, which became mud mixed with litter in the rain. When it rained hard the ground filled up with water and the worms had to come out so they wouldn't drown, Gus said. Some of them wound up crawling onto the sidewalk or the street, and since they were blind there was no way they were going to figure out where they were. We learned more than baseball from Gus. None of us had ever been told about worms in school.

"It's not their fault that we cover up their world with cement," he said. "They're just lost."

"Man, you must be crazy," the guys in the bar would shout out through the open door. And then, safely inside away from the rain, they would add that worms are dirty and how could anyone touch them? "Never shake hands with Gus. Ha, ha. The goof."

We used to get mad at those who made fun of Gus, but he told us to forget it because it didn't bother him. Our parents said to stay away from him because he was strange and possibly unclean. "And don't let him touch you," they would say. "He's dirty." But he was almost a professional ball player and he didn't think he was above us.

Then one day a guy from the bar walked outside and, in full view of his friends inside, stepped on a worm right in front of Gus. And Gus did the only thing he could do. He punched the guy. And he got arrested and charged with assault. He told the police and later told a judge that he had done it to protect a worm.

"You can't protect a worm," they said. "Worms don't have rights."

He was given a suspended sentence and told not to hit anyone else.

"See how crazy your friend is," the adults would say. "He almost went to jail for a worm."

But we didn't think he was crazy at all. In fact, that's when we started having doubts about the people who call others crazy. And that may be the moment when we all started to grow up. After all, Gus was only teaching us about a game he couldn't play and picking up some little creatures that couldn't see, but other people were making fun of him because of that. We knew who was crazy, and it wasn't Gus.

One day not long after that, we were hanging out in front of the bar when Gus's sister left her house to go to work. The guys at the bar strolled over to the window as she got closer. We stood up from the curb and went somewhere too. We joined Gus's sister in her walk.

"Can we go with you to the subway?" we asked. "We want to learn about the phone company."

We passed by the bar and the men's faces in the window and we ignored them, and she was smiling and talking to us. "I'm glad you talk to Gus," she said to us. "He tells me every morning that you are the best friends he has in the whole world."

Unforgettable Fashion

So many things take place in a person's life that there should be a lot to remember. There should be. But that is not the way it really happens. The truth is, you remember only the very few moments when you were at the edge of triumph or disaster. Then you try to forget the disasters.

I was just thinking of my cousin, whose name is Richard and whom everyone calls Dick, and whom I have not seen in decades. For a few years when I was small, I lived with him and his parents and I really looked up to him. He was taller, he was older and he was smarter. He was in grade seven when I was in grade three, and in grade seven, he said, they learned things that grade threes could never imagine.

I was having trouble with long division; he was doing fractions. I was struggling through comic books; he was reading books without pictures. He was my hero.

But then came the incident that made him a real person to me. The day I learned he wasn't perfect. That was the day fashion came to our neighbourhood. At least it was the first time I ever saw anyone interact with their clothes in some way other than just putting them on.

Dick told me it was cool to write your name on the inside of the peak of your baseball cap, so that when you turned it up everyone knew you were Vinnie or Tommy or Jimmy. Of course everyone knew your name already, but in the rare event that you met someone new, they would not say, "Hey, stupid," or "You, dummy," because they could read who you really were.

So Dick pulled out his pen and entered the world of wearable design. He went to a mirror with his hat still on his head, reached up and started to write on the upturned bill. It was a struggle. It is hard to hold a pen over your head and write, especially by watching in the mirror. Very slowly he wrote D-i-c-k.

But all I could see were some lines that looked like letters written backwards. "I don't think that's right," I said.

"You're not old enough to do this," he said.

He took off his hat to admire it, but his face twisted into a kind of question mark. Then he said he knew what was wrong. We couldn't read it this way because we weren't looking at him the way others would see him. He put it back on and stood in front of the mirror. "There, see?" he said. "This is the way other people see it."

I took out a pen too and wrote my name on my cap, but I had it in my lap and I wrote my name just as I would write it on a piece of paper. I could read it, but Dick said no one else would be able to when I had it on my head.

He told me to put it on and stand in front of a mirror and I would see what he meant. We stood side by side and I could see he *was* right. I could read D-i-c-k when I looked at his cap in the mirror, but mine was unreadable: e-k-i-M, which not only looked funny, it looked like Greek, and no one in my family could read that.

Then we went outside and walked into the crowd with the peaks of our caps turned up. Most people ignored us, but a few laughed. Dick hit me in the ribs with his elbow.

"Ha," he said. A "ha" from him could really hurt.

A few more people stared and passed. A few others laughed, and they seemed to be looking more at Dick than at me. He took off his cap and held it out in front of him and pretended that he was walking down the street and just noticing it. Then he looked at my cap. Then he looked back at his.

"I think you're right," he said.

Me? Right?! Wow! In the eyes of my cousin, who was fourteen inches taller than me, I was right! That was a moment that became a treasure. I was right in the eyes of my cousin who could do anything.

He could not rub off the ink so he never wore that cap again, and since he did not wear his I did not wear mine. But my head was too big for it anyway.

That was virtually a lifetime ago. Families have come and gone. Careers have started and ended. But the next time we meet I will ask him about the hat. And the first thing he will say to me is, "I don't remember that at all."

Picking Up the Pails

You know about role models, those kind, hard-working, romantic, generous, rich people that you hope your kids will follow. You have never met a role model, because every time you think you've found one he turns out to be a pedophile or an embezzler, but you still say you want your kids to have good role models to learn from.

In our neighbourhood, most of the mothers told us which people to avoid. There were lots of names on that list, starting with every other kid on the block. And especially we were warned not to grow up like our fathers. Fathers were people who went to war, came home from war and then spent most of their time in bars, talking about the war.

But despite the odds, we did know people whom we wanted to be like. None of us, at least not the boys, had any doubt that we wanted to be garbage men. They were the only people we saw who actually had jobs, as we understood the word. And the biggest benefit of that job, at least for a boy, was that it made you strong.

Over and over we watched the garbage men pick up loaded steel cans and slam them into the back of the truck.

They could put a deep dent in a can on its first day at the curb. You had to be strong to do that.

There was something else they could do: they could whistle. It wasn't a musical whistle, but a pulling back of the lips to emit a sharp, shrill sound that pierced the noise of traffic and banging cans and the radio in the cab of the truck. This whistle would tell the driver to pull ahead another twenty feet. It was a useful whistle, and we spent hours trying to do it, but we only produced a lot of wind and sometimes saliva on our chins.

Then there was a summer day when we made our dream come true. We weren't going to wait to be garbage men. We weren't going to wait until we finished grade ten and then took a civil service test. We were going to be garbage men now. Early one morning, when the truck turned the corner onto our street, the workers found seven dirty-faced kids standing at the first row of cans.

"We want to help," we told them.

"You gotta be kiddin'," one of the men said. "You couldn't lift dese cans."

"And besides," said the other one, who held a cigar in his teeth, "you don't got no Teamster cards."

They were all proud members of the union. The Teamsters controlled the airports, the waterfront, the pizza industry and the garbage trucks.

"My fadda's a Teamster," said Vinnie.

Vinnie didn't have any idea what a Teamster was, but any time anyone said they were something, anything—Swedish, Albino, Catholic, Jew, Teamster—Vinnie would automatically say he or someone in his family was the same thing.

"So your fadda's a Teamster," said the guy with the cigar. This made all the difference. This was the son of a union brother. This was someone who could walk in his footsteps. "Come on, grab a pail."

For the next half hour we dragged cans heavier than ourselves off the curb. We'd had a little experience because all of us had the job at home of putting out the garbage. But none of us had ever before handled cans that were filled with bones. We knew that some families butchered their own meat, but we didn't know that bones could weigh so much, or stink so bad. There was also a lot of household slop, and a lot of unspeakable goop that had to be dumped out of the cans that day. By the time we were halfway along the block, the two Teamster brothers were walking along-side of us and we were doing all the work. Mostly they just whistled and pointed to the cans. They kept telling Vinnie he would make a good Teamster.

At the end of the block they hopped on the back of the truck and took off. We collapsed on the curb and sat there with our arms quivering and our tee shirts and pants soaked with stuff we didn't want to touch.

"I don't want to be a garbage man," said Vinnie.

It is good to learn some of life's lessons early. Vinnie was one of the few kids in that neighbourhood who stayed in school and eventually got a job where he wore a clean shirt. And he was one of the even fewer people who, when the custodian came around to empty his wastebasket, always said thanks.

Cupid Pushed the Pedals

It wasn't Valentine's Day. Flowers and candy were far from anyone's thoughts. The only things being offered that day were sweat and grease and dirt, and the aching need not to lose to a stranger.

It happened a couple of blocks from our street, on a vacant lot next to the post office mail sorting plant. We had races on our bicycles on that lot almost every day. We would pedal in a circle with dust flying out behind our bikes and kids on the sidelines cheering and fixing their bikes for the next race.

Our bikes were built to look like the cars of the day. They were fat and bulky, with lots of chrome. Even the cheapest models were decorated with strips of shiny metal that went around the swollen piece of tin between your knees that was supposed to look like a gas tank. There were no gears. To go faster you had to push harder.

Freddy was the undisputed champ. He was strong and he loved speed and he had his bike so oiled that it was dripping before a race. The other kids put playing cards into the spokes and fastened them to the frame with clothespins so that the bikes would sound like they had motors. But not Freddy, he was there for speed, not for show.

One day a new kid moved into the neighbourhood. His name was Teddy, or at least that is how we understood the English translation, and we weren't sure if we liked him. He was from someplace that had "slav" in its name, and maybe there was an "ick," which we thought was funny. None of us knew much about Europe and less about eastern Europe, so we had no idea where he came from. On the other hand he could find his old country on a map and he knew where he was living now and he spoke two languages, or at least he was learning a second one. Sometimes we saw him walking to the grocery store with his mother, and we saw him in the schoolyard, but we weren't friendly with him because he wasn't friendly with us. He didn't speak enough English to have a conversation with us, and when he talked with his older brother we didn't understand what they were saying and that made us feel like outsiders.

But one day Teddy showed up at the vacant lot. He had a stripped-down bike with no fenders and no kickstand and no tin tank between his knees. He stood by himself for a while, then slowly walked his bike toward a group of us.

"Can I," and he pointed to the track, "me?"

He didn't say hello. He didn't even nod his head.

"Maybe," we said. "You think you're fast enough?"

Teddy shrugged, and stared at us. He understood something, maybe the word *fast*, or maybe he only understood "maybe."

One kid drew a line across the track with his heel. "You against Freddy," the kid said. "Ten laps." And then, to make sure Teddy understood, the kid held out both hands with all the fingers up.

"Go!"

They started by standing on their pedals, the full weight of their bodies going down on the chain. Freddy aimed for the inside track. Teddy was in there too. Their bikes almost touched. One lap around and we were all yelling. Freddy's little sister Eileen was on the sidelines too. She loved her big brother and she was shouting, "Go! Go!" with the rest of us.

Two, three laps and it was nose to nose. Both riders were leaning over their handlebars. The wind had blown off Freddy's cap.

The postal workers in the big sorting plant came out on their lunch break and they started shouting too. I saw some money passing hands. They were betting on the bikes.

"Look!" I poked a kid who was standing next to me. "This is a big race."

"I bet they're betting on Freddy," he said. "I'll bet you too. I'll bet you he wins."

"But I bet he wins too," I said.

"Well then, I bet the other kid loses," he said.

"OK, how much?"

The two of them flew by, leaving a wake of dust that settled on our shoes.

"I don't have any money," the other kid said, "but I bet Freddy's going to win anyway."

The eighth lap, and I know we were shouting, but it seemed quiet. I watched Teddy's bike creep up on Freddy's, even though Teddy was on the outside. He had to go farther, he had to go faster, he had to push harder.

"Go Freddy! Go!" We couldn't let a foreign kid who couldn't speak English beat us. "Go Freddy!"

The tenth lap, and we were screaming. I watched the two of them come up to the finish line wheel to wheel. Both their faces were ready to explode. Then they were across the line.

"Freddy won, Freddy won!" we shouted.

"No," the postal workers shouted over to us. "It was a tie!"

"Wasn't," we shouted back. "Freddy won."

"A tie," they said.

Freddy and Teddy were on the ground wheezing like broken engines, their faces too dirty and exhausted to show either pride or dejection.

"You won, Freddy," we said. "You won."

Then a small voice came from the back of the crowd. "Teddy came first," it said. It was Eileen. "I saw him beat my brother by this much," and she held up her fingers showing two inches. "It's not fair to say Freddy won."

We never knew who had won. It was a photo finish and we had no camera. But strange things happen when people try with all their might to do something. Freddy and Teddy became the best of friends, and stayed that way after they became Fred and Ted and after Fred had an accident on a motorcycle ten years later. They still go out together and they watch a lot of little league baseball and soccer games. Fred sits in a wheelchair and he and Ted talk about who the best runners are. Fred always says the fastest one is his own nephew, who was named Freddy after him, and who is Ted and Eileen's son.

The vacant lot is gone now. A bowling alley was built on our racetrack. But one thing has not changed: next Valentine's Day, as on all Valentine's Days, Ted will give Eileen a card, which will have a variation on the same picture that he has always given her. He spends weeks each year looking for the right card. It is not a Valentine's Day card; it is one of those general-purpose blank cards. But always the one he chooses has a bicycle on the front, and he draws a heart around it.

Hunting for Submarines

There is something missing in school nowadays. Do you know how many kids can't tie their shoelaces or tell time on a watch that has Mickey Mouse on the dial? Shoelaces have been replaced by Velcro, which may keep your shoes on, but you never get a chance to trip on your own laces. And with digital readouts there are kids who don't know what time it is when Mickey's big hand is on the twelve and his little hand is on the three. They will become adults without ever fumbling through childhood.

There is one other skill that has almost completely disappeared. There are people in their twenties who have never, ever, with their own hands washed a sink full of dishes. Cleaning up means putting plates in a rack in a machine. But when you do it that way, you miss the adventures waiting in the sudsy water.

In days gone by, you could find those adventures at the end of a game called You Can't Go Out Until You Do the Dishes. That was a contest in which your mother was the opposition team as well as the judge and the referee. It began when you finished dinner and felt your mother's eyes on you as you looked longingly at the door.

"You're not going anywhere, young man, until you get those dishes done."

That was the starting bell for the game. It rang in all the houses in the neighbourhood at about the same time. Everyone ate dinner at around six, and at six-thirty the dish game began.

"Can't I go out and do them later, please, Mom, please, just this once, please. Joey's got a new set of baseball cards and he wants me to see them."

"Not until you finish the dishes."

Darn, there goes your mother spoiling all the fun. So you stand there, barely tall enough to get your arms over the edge of the sink. You have stood there every night since you had to climb onto a chair to reach. This was the one universal job for kids. If you had younger brothers or sisters, you could bribe them or threaten them, but only until your mother found out, and then it was your job again.

So you piled the dishes into the sink and filled it with water and soap and pushed up your sleeves and dove your hands into the bubbles. You started moving the dishrag around on the plates and cups and suddenly there were submarines down there, and you had to hunt for them. One of them was hiding on the other side of the sunken shipwrecks. That was the enemy sub, your left hand.

And you were the good guys in another submarine on the other side of the sink. You moved that sub around carefully with the water flowing over your arm and your fingers feeling their way through the underwater obstacles. But you could never see them, because no one in a submarine could see anything. So you closed your eyes and prowled the bottom of the endless sea and one sub tried to outma-noeuvre the other, behind the plates and under the tangle of wrecked ships that were disguised as knives and forks.

Then the subs surfaced for air, but still they were hiding from each other in the bubbles. And just as you were about to fire the torpedoes and win the war, you heard, "Hurry up with those dishes or you won't be able to go out." Darn, there goes your mother, spoiling all the fun again.

"Can I go out now and finish them later?"

"No."

So you finished washing those dishes and went out and bragged about washing them so fast that your mother bare-ly noticed when you were done.

School programs should go back to basics. Reading and writing are important, but not being able to wash dishes is a serious educational deficit. For one thing, it means kids will grow up and never know what it is like to pilot a submarine.

The Deli

It was filled with the smells of baloney and salami and ham and cheese. And there was always hot homemade soup, and you could buy coleslaw and milk and bread and really, what else do you need?

The deli was the best store, the sidewalk oasis, and when I was small my mother would send me there after she got home from work. It was always the same thing that I was told to buy: four hot dogs, a half pound of potato salad and a good tomato.

"Make sure," my mother would say, "that the tomato is ripe. Tell them to give you a firm one."

This was not a neighbourhood where there were steaks. But there were tomatoes, and we were not going to settle for anything but the best.

But this story is not about food. It is about the couple who ran the deli, Abe and Golda. They were so happy, all the time. Golda had grey hair and a smile that could warm the steel pillars of the elevated train that ran right outside their front door. The train was so noisy that when it passed, you couldn't hear a shout inside the store. And the tracks overhead kept the sun out. But the sunshine was inside.

Abe was always joking. He would say something funny about a quarter pound of sliced cheese or the coins on the counter and he would joke about his wife and the weather and taxes. And he would give everyone a compliment, even me. He would call me a gentleman and a scholar. It didn't matter that he said that to everyone. I was ten years old, wearing a torn sweater and a dirty face, and I was treated with unreserved honour and dignity.

Sometimes I was wrestling with a problem, with my mother, or with other kids, or with school, or with the nightmares that kids have, and they would see it in my face and say, "Don't worry, things always get better." And I would believe them.

They would send me away with a dill pickle that they picked out of a jar and didn't charge me for. Every time I eat a pickle now, I am back in that store.

There was one other thing about this couple. No one ever said anything to them about it and they never talked about it, at least I never heard it discussed and I was in there hundreds of times over a half dozen years.

This hard-working couple with their smiles and their jokes both had long, ugly numbers tattooed on their forearms. We all knew what it meant, but we didn't talk about it. We didn't ask, how much did you suffer? Or, what was it like? Or, how did you survive? We just saw the warm, smiling faces and we heard the jokes and the laughter, and so many times I heard those words: "Don't worry, things always get better."

Sewer Fishing

Jimmy Lee was a great fisherman. He was born in the city, he had never seen a lake or a pond, but he was a true fisherman, and my best friend. He lived across the alley and we strung up a tin can phone between our bedroom windows.

He would come to the back of my house early in the morning, knock on the window until I was awake, then say, "I'm going to call you." Then he walked home, opened his window and shouted to me, "Are you ready to talk?"

I opened my window, stuck out my head and shouted back, "OK, I'm here. Pick up the phone."

The phone was made of two tin cans attached by a long string that was knotted inside each can. If we both pulled on our cans, we could talk.

"OK, I'm going to talk," shouted Jimmy. "You put the can against your ear."

"I want to talk," I shouted back. "You talked last time."

"First I talk, then you talk," he shouted back.

I held the can against my ear and heard a vibration that I couldn't understand. So I put the can to my mouth and said into it, "I don't understand you."

"Youcan'ttallkwhileI'mtalking," Jimmy said. I could only hear part of it because my mouth was in the can and his words were coming across my cheeks before they got to my ears. But he always said the same thing, so I knew what it was. After that he always said, "Canyouhearme?"

"You're pulling too hard," I shouted into the can. I was struggling to hold on to it because Jimmy was stronger than me.

He leaned farther out his window. "Let's go fishing," he said.

Jimmy loved fishing, and he stuck with it long after the rest of us got bored because we weren't catching anything. As soon as Jimmy got home from school he would take out his string and a pin and walk over to the fishing hole and spend an hour. People passing by would laugh and say, "There's no fish down there, are you nuts?" Jimmy would look up and say, "You're wrong. There's a fish down there and I'm going to catch it."

The fishing had started one winter day when we went into Tommy Taggart's house to get out of the cold and someone saw a soup bowl full of water sitting on the kitchen table. Inside the bowl was a tiny fish, not actually swimming because there wasn't enough room to move, but its gills were going and its fins and tail waved in the water, and that was amazing. "My mother won it at bingo," Tommy said.

No one on that street had a pet. We had no dogs because who was going to buy extra meat to feed a dog when the family was eating macaroni and cheese? And no cats because we were always told that if you can't take a pet out for a walk, there's no sense in having it. ("But that doesn't mean we're getting a dog!")

We looked down at the bowl and Dorothy asked, "What do you do with a fish?"

"I don't know. I think you look at it," said Tommy.

So five kids with their elbows on the table and their hands holding up their chins stared at one fish that had nowhere to go.

"Gee, that's neat," said Jimmy. "It's really alive, you can even see it breathing."

It was one of our first discoveries of nature: some things are alive. In a world of concrete and plasterboard, this was a major find.

"I wonder if it eats things?" someone asked.

We got a slice of bread and dropped little pinches in the water, but the fish ignored them. Then we tried lettuce, but no luck. We got some baloney from the refrigerator, but still the fish would not eat.

"Maybe we should take it outside for some fresh air," said Vinnie.

We held our breath while we carried it. This fish was a precious thing. Within minutes, word had spread through the neighbourhood and kids were crowding around to get a look in the bowl. And then someone wanted to pet it, and a few of the boys got to pushing and shoving, as boys do, and before we knew it, the bowl flipped over. We just happened to be standing near a sewer, and the contents of the bowl, including the fish, went down through the steel grating. We could hear the water splashing into the darkness down below the street.

"My mother's going to kill me," said Tommy.

"We'll get it back," said Dorothy.

She ran home and came back with safety pins and string, and we spent the rest of that day lowering hooks into the black hole. When someone wanted to park his car over the grate we told him no, we were fishing for Tommy's mother's fish. The driver didn't argue. Confronted by kids as determined as we were, he probably figured his car would be safer if he squeezed it back and left the sewer uncovered. We sat on the ground just in front of his bumper. Now we had a fishing hole with a backrest.

"I got it," Jimmy said. "I got a bite."

"You're kidding."

"No, really!"

He struggled to pull up the line. Something was fighting back.

"Jimmy's got the fish. He's got the fish!" You could hear us yelling at the end of the block.

"It's hurting my finger."

"Careful it doesn't get away."

"It's wiggling."

Jimmy pulled and we held our breath.

"It's coming," he said. "It's coming up. Someone grab it."

I was closest. I pushed my hand and arm between the iron bars and reached around. "I got it," I said. "Oh damn, oh yuck." It wasn't a fish. I pulled it up between the bars. It was a piece of chicken wire fencing with several condoms snagged in it. "Yuck, damn," I said, and dropped it. Someone else kicked it down the street.

"I'm going to get that fish," Jimmy said, and when he said that, he became a fisherman.

For the next few years Jimmy and I went fishing every couple of days, whenever there was no car parked over the sewer. We caught some more condoms and a few pieces of clothing, but we never got that fish.

Sometimes people walking past would laugh and ask if we were fishing for rats.

"No," Jimmy would say. "Fish."

"There's no fish down there," they would say.

Jimmy would look up in defiance. "You just wait. You'll see."

When we became teenagers, Jimmy started dating a girl named Margie, who came from another neighbourhood. He told her and her friends that he was a fisherman, and since they had never met a fisherman he became a guy with a mysterious past. Sometimes that is all you need to be popular. He hung out a lot with Margie and before he finished high school he proposed to her. He asked me to be his best man. I was seventeen.

What I remember most about his wedding was that the day before it I got a shave from the barber on the corner of our street. I had never had a professional shave before and I spent the entire night before Jimmy's wedding lying awake in bed rubbing my face on the pillow, trying to take away the burning. Getting married was painful.

"You look terrible," he said to me at the church.

"My face is on fire."

Throughout the ceremony I held my hands at my sides while my cheeks ached to be touched. The burning is all I remember of the exchanging of vows.

For their honeymoon, Jimmy and Margie went to a country resort and went fishing every day. He had become what he wanted to be. Then they had two kids, and even when they were babies he took them fishing. A few years later, when I was twenty-three and serving in the air force, I got a letter saying that Jimmy had died of a heart attack. It was a congenital problem. He was a year older than me.

I read in the letter that the funeral procession had driven down our old street, which means it passed the sewer where we fished. I know Jimmy's spirit looked at that hole in the asphalt where he and I had talked about things that have meaning, like life, and death, and hooking the fish that he really, truly wanted to return to the bowl in Tommy's mother's kitchen.

THE RESCUE MISSION

The school was overcrowded. The smaller kids had to sit two to a seat. Those were the old-fashioned school desks where the seats and the desks were bolted to the floor and stood in straight rows from the front of the classroom to the back wall.

At lunchtime the poor kids were lined up on one side of the basement, which was the gymnasium when it wasn't a lunchroom. "All those who get free lunch, go stand against the wall." That was the announcement, made without concern about stigmas or hurt feelings. Then, one at a time, each kid was given a peanut butter and jelly sandwich wrapped in wax paper and a small container of milk in a waxed carton. The milk was always room temperature and had bits of wax floating in it that had come away from the container. After lunch you could spit the wax at other kids.

This story is about food, but none that was eaten. One day a young teacher, Miss Johnson, wanted to show us how plants drink water. There is history in that sentence, because these events took place in an age when woman teachers were not allowed to be married, and because teaching us something about plants would be novel—no plants sat on the windowsills of any school back then.

But in that grade four class, kids were trying to push each other out of their single seats and few of us heard what she said. The class quieted down when she took a stick of celery out of a bag. You were not allowed to bring food into class. And then we all went silent when she poured ink into a jar and then put the celery into the ink.

"You will now see how the ink rises up in the veins of the celery," said Miss Johnson.

"You can't do that, Miss Johnson," said about twenty kids, and a bunch more wanted to say it. Thirty-six kids all had the same thought, the thought of drinking ink. All thirty-six tried not to swallow.

"It will only take a short time," said Miss Johnson. "Celery is very thirsty."

Thirty-six kids curled up their tongues and pulled in their cheeks in sympathy and leaned forward over their desks. In those days you were not allowed to leave your seat without permission, even in the early grades of elementary school.

One hand went up. Usually there were no questions about anything. Then three hands were up. Then ten.

Miss Johnson smiled with obvious pleasure and pointed to one kid. "Yes?"

"Miss Johnson, that's mean and cruel making that celery drink ink."

Oh, no, she told us, we shouldn't worry about that. It was just a piece of celery and we would learn something. But there is a wide gap between theories of education and life as nine-year-olds see it.

Ten minutes later Miss Johnson told us that we could come to the front of the classroom one row at a time and observe the wonders of science. There were ughs and yucks from the first kids on the scene. By the time the fourth row was called to look, the class was in mourning for the celery. Every face was down.

Miss Johnson was a nice woman, and she was just doing what the lesson plan had called for, and our reaction was not in the plan. However, it was a lesson many of us would never forget.

One kid had to go to the bathroom and got a bathroom pass from Miss Johnson while the fifth and last row of kids were attending the wake for the celery. They crowded around the table and gazed sadly at the jar. "Poor celery," they said. "We're sorry."

The bathroom kid came back, carefully holding something behind his back and squeezed in with the other kids at the table for one last look. By the time all the kids were back in their seats, everyone looked happy. Miss Johnson looked confused, perhaps because she was new to teaching and she knew she had much to learn.

"So, class, do we understand now how a piece of celery drinks?"

She turned to pick up the jar and there, on the table, was the stick of celery in a jar filled with fresh, clean water.

If we had been shocked by Miss Johnson's ill-use of an innocent stick of celery, we were even more shocked at what happened next. She asked no one any questions and she reprimanded no one. She only smiled and said, "Tomorrow we are going to plant some seeds in a pot and see what happens."

I have a feeling Miss Johnson became a very fine teacher, and I know thirty-six grade four kids learned one important thing that day: if you stop bad things from happening you'll have good things to remember.

Party Animals

"No one's going to be home?" Vinnie asked, trying to hold back his grinning smile because it was too good to be true.

"I mean it, no one," said Johnny.

"And we can get away with it?"

"We just have to ask them."

This was after we were done being kids but we weren't grownups yet, and before we left the neighbourhood and drifted apart and got married and went into the army, and before some of us died. This was when life was so exciting we could barely contain ourselves, and so boring we could not stand it. This was when we were fourteen and had pimples and when we loved to party. But there was always one problem with the parties. The parents never left us alone.

Except this time, when Johnny Martin's parents were visiting his mother's sister and they would have to stay there overnight and Johnny was left at home because Johnny had to go to school. Johnny could not believe what he was hearing.

"Oh, I'll be good," he said.

His parents drove away and Johnny went out on the street and met Vinnie and they felt that the window of opportunity had just been pulled wide open, as it is on the first warm day of spring when the stale inside air is washed away. The stale air was the parties we usually had, the kind where the girls would invite us and we would find clean shirts and wash our faces and with our parents' blessings we would go. You know what kind of party that is going to be.

All the boys would walk down the street, meeting each other on the way, and we would all say the same thing: "Do you think her parents are going to be home?"

"Of course they're going to be home," someone else would say. "You don't think Judy's mother would trust us, do you?"

But that is what we hoped for, dreamed about: a party when we would be alone with the girls. With no parents around we could—well, you know. After all, there would be no parents around and, wow, you know.

Then we would walk into Judy's house and there would be Judy and Eileen and Dorothy and Vanessa and a few others, and behind them Judy's mother, and coming into the room would be Judy's father, who drove a moving truck. We would say, "Hello, Mrs. Tracy," because we were all polite. But we would think, Would you please go into the next room for a while, Mrs. Tracy? But she never did. She disappeared only for a minute at a time to get more pop or chips, and what can you do in a minute?

We also wished for slow dances so we could snuggle and breathe deeply, but Mrs. Tracy seemed to have organized the records so that only fast music was available, and the girls were the only ones who could dance to that. So the boys just stood around talking about baseball and the cars they hoped someday to own.

But this night would be different. Johnny's parents were gone and the dirty space below the first floor in his home would be the party room of our dreams. His basement was rough. It had some old coal bins that had never been cleaned out, even after an oil furnace was installed. It had a bare concrete floor, and bare light bulbs and an overflow sewer drain that had overflowed several times and then dried. But it didn't matter. The girls would be here without any parents.

The girls started arriving shortly after sunset. They had told their parents that they were going out for chips and Cokes with their friends, and seven of them showed up. We were waiting like hungry puppies, falling over each other, wrestling and talking about what we hoped would happen. We had a six-pack of beer for twelve of us.

"Are you sure your mother's not home?" Vanessa asked.

"We could run around naked and no one would know," said Johnny.

"Who would do that?" asked Vanessa, in a tone that left Johnny wishing he had just said no, his mother was not home, but he hadn't said that. He had said something that would probably cause Vanessa not to talk to him for the rest of the night.

The girls brought a stack of records and we had a 45-rpm player with a three-inch speaker in the side. It would make music we could squeeze by. We were aching to start. Then the girls put on a record by Elvis: "Hound Dog."

"Hey, we can't dance to that," Tommy tried to shout over the music, but the girls were already dancing, ignoring us. We stood by the coal bins with our hands in our pockets.

"The next one will be slow," said Tommy. "They're just burning off their excitement."

But the next selection was "Jail House Rock." It was the age of early Elvis.

"Hey, can't you put on a slow one?" Vinnie shouted, but the girls didn't listen and didn't stop dancing. He and Tommy looked through the records, flipping them down like a deck of cards. "Fast, fast, fast, fast."

Then Tommy's hands stopped. He pulled out a record and held it in the air like a trophy. "'Love Me Tender'," he said. When "Stagger Lee" finished, he put on Elvis to hug by, and to grope and get excited by.

"Love me tender, tender, tender, tender." He nudged it past the scratch, and Elvis sang, "Love me true, true, true, true." You can't snuggle with a scratched record.

"I think I hear your mother upstairs," said Jimmy Lee.

"No, that's the mice. When I come down here they run around up there," said Johnny.

Then came the beer. It was warm. We had to carry it in one can at a time inside our shirts in case someone spotted us, so when we opened the first can it had already travelled a block squeezed between a belly and a belt and getting shaken with every step. When the can opener went in, the beer came out—up to the ceiling and down over Judy's hair.

"Aaahhhgh!" Judy did not like beer on her head. "Oh, God, I can't go home like this."

The other girls stopped dancing and huddled around her as if she were a wounded ally. They got towels and tried to dry the hair, then they got water and tried to wet it. They scrubbed and combed and circled her, comforting her and

101

talking about whatever it is that girls talk about. I could not hear what they said because I was on the other side of the room with the boys, talking about baseball and the cars that we hoped someday to own.

But the next day, when we sat on the curb watching the traffic go by, things were different. A failure? A bomb? No way.

"What a party! Wow!" said Vinnie.

"Wild," said Tommy.

"You know, when Judy had that towel on her head, she looked pretty," said Johnny.

And the best part was that we could have another party soon because we still had five beers stashed behind the furnace. All we had to do was wait for Johnny's parents to visit his mother's sister again. The only potential problem was that Johnny overheard his father saying he couldn't stand his sister-in-law. But if he changed his mind and the girls were willing and we could find a slow record and find a way to chill the beer, we would have a time that you couldn't believe.

Something else had happened that night. We saw a picture of Elvis on one of the record labels. Over his pouting face was a magnificent pomp of hair. It hung almost to his eyebrows like a dark cloud.

"Looks like poop," Vinnie said when he saw the girls aahing over it.

So, on this day while we sat on the curb watching the trucks go by, Vinnie stuck his fingers into the front of his hair and pulled it down.

"What are you doing?" asked Johnny.

"Nothing."

"You're trying to look like Elvis," said Tommy.

"Am not."

"Are so."

"Not."

"Yes you are," said Tommy. "I want to look like that too."

"Me too," said Vinnie.

We chipped in and got a tube of Brylcreem, which we squeezed out like car grease. Each of us smeared a glob on our heads, which made us look like ball joints ready to be slid into sockets. When we shook our heads, our hair stayed glued. We all pulled plops down over our foreheads and asked each other if we looked like Elvis.

No, we did not look like him. No sideburns. So we went to the barber, who told us that we would not have sideburns until we had whiskers. "And you won't have those," he said, "until you start liking girls."

"I like girls," said Vinnie.

"I mean really like girls," said the barber.

"What do you mean 'really'?" asked Vinnie, who had images of Vanessa almost naked in his mind.

"If you have to ask what I mean, you're not old enough to know what I mean and you're not old enough to have sideburns."

This was one of the mysteries of life. We found a cork and burned it, and the next day we all had sideburns. We spent the next year anointing our heads with grease and singing "Hound Dog" and "Blue Suede Shoes." As it happened, during that year some of us had to use less and less cork and we spent more and more time talking to Vanessa and Dorothy than singing on the corner under the street light. That was another mystery of life.

We never had that second party, and worse than that, when we went to look for the beer a few months later it was gone. Johnny hadn't taken it and no one else could get into his cellar. Except, he remembered, for the day when the furnace broke down and his Uncle Ed came to fix it. His uncle could fix anything and he was really quick. But this time he spent a long time in the cellar, and when he finished he ran to the bathroom upstairs.

"I like cream soda better anyway," said Johnny. So we got a can of that from the corner store and sat on the curb talking about girls and Elvis and parties as we passed the can around, and none of us ever wiped off the mouth of the can before we drank. We didn't have to. We were buddies who partied together.

A Razor at the Throat

There is a turning point for a kid when he is no longer a kid, when he becomes a guy, and everyone knows that corner is turned when hormones begin to squirt. But if you are thinking about the effects on the lower parts of the body, wrong. The big change takes place on the chin, and that change causes a normal boy to take a sharp piece of metal to his face and neck and try not to kill himself.

I had the good luck to be in attendance at Vinnie's first shave. He had watched his father for weeks, and now he was ready. He lathered his face and I sat on the edge of the bathtub in awe.

"I saved one of my father's old blades," Vinnie said.

We all start with the belief that dull blades won't hurt as much. Big mistake. He had barely taken it out of the envelope when he cut his thumb.

"Yow!" He held it under running water, which made it look like he was losing even more blood. "I'm going to die," he said, "and I haven't even shaved yet."

We found a styptic pencil in the medicine cabinet. They are supposed to stop the bleeding, but what they really do is make you feel like a hornet is jabbing its stinger into your finger. Vinnie shrieked and jumped and I wished that I wouldn't grow up too soon. Eventually, with half a roll of toilet paper wrapped around his finger, he managed to stop the bleeding.

Then he put the razor to his face. "Ouch!" He cut himself on the first stroke. His shaving cream turned pink. He took some more toilet paper, but it got soggy and you can't stop bleeding with wet paper. Finally he was able to take another stroke with the razor, and he cut himself again. His face looked like pink cotton candy and the only reason he didn't quit was that I was watching. So he put one of his fingers in front of the blade so that he could finish shaving without allowing the razor to actually touch his face.

He rinsed, which started the bleeding again. Then he dried with more toilet paper and put three bandages on his cheeks and another around his thumb. Then he went outside and one of the neighbourhood girls said, "Poor you. That must hurt."

"Naaah," said Vinnie. "I didn't even notice it. It's just part of being a guy."

THE BOOKIE

When the government got into gambling, it did two bad things. It made it too easy, and it took away the romance. Easy gambling is bad. We can gamble anywhere—at the supermarket, the gas station and at casinos that are multiplying as fast as the losses at the slot machines. But the worst part is the romance. There is none at the lottery counter. There is no secrecy, no sense of guilt or worry about being caught. Gambling now is just a bad business transaction with the government.

It didn't always work that way. For instance, there was Abe the Irishman. Abe was Jewish and Irish Catholic, which everyone knew was a combination that made him sharp, tough, potentially corrupt, warm and kind. "And that is just on one side," said Abe.

Abe the Irishman was a bookie. He worked at a dry cleaner's a few blocks from the neighbourhood. His customers leaned over the counter and he sat on the other side with a needle and thread in his hand and a cigar in his mouth. He kept sewing in case the police came in. He sewed the same piece of material for months until it was round and fat with threads. As soon as he saw a customer, he would drop the needle and pick up his notebook. You gave him the name of the team, he gave you the odds, you gave him the money.

The dry cleaner's was a very popular place in the neighbourhood. Most of the men dropped in there a couple of times a week to check on the state of their pants or jackets, and while they were there they might have the inclination to place a little wager: baseball, football, it didn't matter what. Every season offered possibilities.

Then one day, one of the mothers went into the cleaner's to tell Abe that his business was ruining their family. It was not because of the gambling, because most of the bets were very small. No one had much money to begin with, and Abe had a five-dollar limit: "We don't want people to lose so much that they can't afford to lose some more." Abe was practical as well as thoughtful.

But all the men in the neighbourhood spent every night and every weekend listening to the games on the radio or, worse yet, getting together to watch sports at the few places that had televisions. "Their kids are on the street and their fathers are inside," said the mother. Mothers, as always with mothers, were too busy caring for the new babies and cleaning and cooking to keep their wings over all their children all the time. "The children need someone to watch them or they might do bad things and turn out to be crooks like you," she said.

"I will think about this problem," said Abe the Irishman, "and I will try to fix it." He wished to be of help, because he was a good man of the community, but he did not wish to give up his livelihood. The solution came while he concentrated on his needle and thread. "You do not need professionals to help you solve problems," Abe always said. "You need only to think hard about them." Then he said, "We will bet no more on professional athletes."

From then on he became the bookmaker for the neighbourhood and for all the nearby neighbourhoods. There were sandlot baseball teams and girls' hopscotch, and rope skipping and stickball and street hockey. Nowadays kids spend their time indoors with video games. But there was an age when playing meant being outdoors, and that is where every kid everywhere in the world who was not doing homework or eating or sleeping grew up. The street was the universal playground and the possibilities were endless. Abe began combing back alleys and street corners and vacant lots, scouting for talented ten-year-olds and teenagers.

In a week he was taking bets on 132nd Street versus 124th Street in touch football, and the kids of Union Congregational Church versus Yeshiva Synagogue in basketball. He gave 5–3 odds on Judy the marble player against the boy who had come on the bus from another neighbourhood to challenge her.

You may think it is a sin to bet on your kids, but to Abe it was good business. And to the parents—well, every parent was putting up dimes and quarters on their kids. No one was watching television. Abe had to hire kids to bring him the scores from the street corners. The entire community was out to watch and wager on every roller skate race down the block.

For one summer we had the excitement of Las Vegas and the spirit of the Stanley Cup every day. But eventually the police raided the dry cleaner's and put Abe out of business. That was when the government was against gambling. Times change.

However, there was something every kid in that neighbourhood got from Abe's business: everyone did very well at arithmetic in school. Any kid could tell you the payoff on an 8-5 bet without blinking. And as far as I know, not a single one of them puts money into the government-run sports lotteries. After all, how can you place a bet with a computer that can't hold a needle and thread?

The Rock

Buster was a rarity on our block. He didn't have any brothers and sisters and he didn't have a father, but when he was about eight, he had an army of clothespins. He would hide the soldiers behind the legs of furniture in his apartment, and when he brought them outside they would become patrols crawling around the cracks of the sidewalk. There were battles to be fought and wars to be won, and until the other kids came out to play Buster was in the platoon of the wooden soldiers.

"Buster, I have to hang up the clothes," said his mother.

"Now?" There was disappointment, but no arguing. She was standing by the window with wet underwear in her hand, and soldiers have duties between battles. So Buster handed over the clothespins and went outside and discovered the rock.

There were plenty of rocks because we lived next to the railroad tracks and the ties and rails were laid in endless ribbons of brown stones. Buster's rock was brown and shaped like a pyramid, except it only had three sides. It was about the size of a plum.

Buster stared at it for a while. Tommy asked him what he was looking at.

"Nothing," Buster said, and he kept on staring.

"Must be something."

"Nope, nothing."

But he kept his eyes on the rock, hardly blinking, and then Vinnie walked by and asked him what he was doing.

"Just pretending," Buster said.

And maybe because they didn't laugh, he quietly told Vinnie and Tommy that there were some people, some farmers, living on the side of the mountain. "You see where those little holes are in the rock? They live in there."

Then Buster added, "The evil king lives at the top and he's taking away all their food."

Vinnie tried hard to see the people. "You're making that up," he said.

"No." Buster looked up in defiance. He didn't want to sound stupid. "They're really small. And the good guys are down at the bottom of the mountain." He talked fast because sometimes that made people think you didn't have time to make it up. "But the guys at the bottom can't climb up the hill fast enough because they haven't eaten for a long time and they're weak."

Tommy and Vinnie were listening and looking.

"And the king's army is just about to take over the farmers' land and throw them out when one of the good guys says he'll save them because he's in love with a girl who lives on the farm," said Buster.

"Then what happened?" asked Tommy.

"The good guy sneaked up the back side of the mountain."

Buster turned the rock around and they all watched as he moved his fingernail slowly up a crevice. "And then he fought off the king's guards and captured the king."

It was as though Vinnie and Tommy were at the movies. They said nothing; they just kept looking at the rock.

"Then the king's army had to go back and try to rescue him," said Buster, "and that gave the good guys at the bottom time to get to the farms and get some food, and then they attacked the bad guys and threw them off the mountain."

Buster might as well have said it was round twelve and the hometown boy won by a knockout.

"And the good guy and the girl got married."

"Did all that really happen?" asked Vinnie.

"Yeah," said Buster, "and then they all went back down to right here and had a feast."

A few days later some bigger boys from another neighbourhood were passing by and saw Buster playing with his rock, and they took it away from him and threw it back on the tracks along with a million other rocks. Later we found out what had happened and we heard that the bigger kids were bragging about how they made this little kid cry. We all went to Buster's house to make him feel better and we found him sitting on his front steps. By then he had wiped away his tears and looked very pleased with himself.

"Those big boys are rotten," we said.

"Doesn't matter," said Buster. "The farmers and the good guys escaped just in time." He turned over his hand and in it was another rock. But it was no ordinary rock. It had cracks and chips in it, and if you looked close enough, Buster said, you could almost see the people deep in the shadows of the valleys.

STUMPY

I'd like to tell you about the time Stumpy joined our gang. He was with us for more than a year and he taught us about relationships and obligations, although we didn't call them relationships and obligations then. Stumpy was tough. Stumpy was a survivor. Stumpy was brave. Stumpy was a pigeon with one foot.

"That's so sad," said Dorothy, the first time we saw him. We were coming home from school and he was lurching around by the curb, trying to pick up crumbs of bread. Every time he would limp toward one, some other pigeon would get it first.

"We should feed him," said Vanessa. We were all ten and eleven then, and unfairness was something we thought we could straighten out. If we could do it with just some bread, it would be done immediately or even quicker, because one of the boys had a cookie in his pocket. He crumbled it up while the rest of us tried to shoo the other birds away. He sprinkled the pieces on the ground for Stumpy, who gobbled them up faster than we could believe. He was hungry.

The next day Stumpy was in the same fix. He was getting outmanoeuvred by the other pigeons.

"He looks so strong," said Johnny. "If that was my foot I couldn't outrun any of you."

We watched Stumpy hobbling bravely on his footless leg in the race for food, but he could not get to the crumbs fast enough. We did not know his name was Stumpy until Dorothy shook her head and said, "Stumpy's not doing so well." The name stuck, and we stayed with him. We fed him more cookies, and the day after that we fed him more cookies.

We wondered how he had lost his foot. It must have been awful. We knew he didn't have any painkillers, and he didn't have any medicine. He didn't even have a way to complain. He became our universal pet. As soon as we got home from school we would find out whether anyone had fed Stumpy, and then someone would run home for some bread. No parent had to remind us that we had a responsibility to take care of our pet. In the winter when it was bitter cold we chipped in together and bought a box of canary seed to feed him.

And we talked about him so much in school that kids from other neighbourhoods came to see him. Some of them were kids we had been fighting with, but when it came to feeding a bird with one foot, we all stood together.

A summer and a winter passed and one day Stumpy wasn't there. Two days and then three went by without Stumpy. We all stood on the corner.

"He's dead," said Vinnie.

"I miss him," said Vanessa.

"He was our friend," said Johnny.

Some of us had been to the funerals of our grandparents. We all saw people die in the movies. We all knew about death. But we all cried, even the boys.

Thirty years later I went to Nanaimo, British Columbia, and I did a story for television about a man who drove twenty miles every morning from his home in Ladysmith, back to the place where he used to live. He carried half a loaf of bread in his car. At the end of his trip was a seagull, waiting for him on the roof of the house that he used to live in. It was standing on just one foot—its only foot.

"That's Stumpy," he told me. He threw some bread on the ground and the bird flew down to get it.

He had started feeding Stumpy when he lived in the house. He felt sorry for him because a seagull with one foot cannot even swim straight, much less outrace other birds on land. When the man moved to a new house in a new city he didn't break Stumpy's trust. Every morning for three years, he drove back to feed him.

"It may sound stupid," he said, "but he needs me and I need him."

Stumpy is not a name given to many pets. No, the name has to be earned, and when it is, it means two things. One: life is hard. Two: friends make it easier.

THE LITTLE RED STOCKING

The cameraman on the story about Stumpy was Don Timbrell, one of the best photographers ever to work at BCTV. After we finished our work we took a side trip to Duncan. "It's where I grew up," he said. We all like to go back to our roots, to our old neighbourhoods, even those who have been in jails and concentration camps, because there are memories that can only be brought back when you are standing in the actual places that shaped who you are.

"That's where I spent most of my early life." Don pointed to a row of long barracks-like buildings that were now abandoned, the Duncan Orphanage.

He was one of the thousands of the children who were sent away from London during the bombings. All he remembers of the war are the screams of the air raid sirens and the explosions and his home being blown to pieces. He was five years old. He remembers crawling under the stairs with his brother right before the bomb hit. He doesn't remember his parents. They did not make it under the stairs.

After that, the orphanage became his family. Two hundred boys and girls lived there, twenty in each dormitory. Each dorm had a housemother, one woman with twenty children. Love and affection were spread thin. Don said that Sunday was the most important day of the week, and not because they went to church. On Sundays all the kids would stand at attention at the foot of their beds, staring straight at the opposite wall, not moving their heads, not moving their arms or hands. Walking along in front of them were adults, looking the kids over, checking heights, faces, fingernails. They were the prospective parents, looking over what was offered, shopping for a child. All the kids, including Don, thought, "Pick me, please pick me." He was there for seven years before someone took him home.

There was one other day to look forward to. Sometime in September the officials at the orphanage would hand out catalogues to the kids. Don did not remember what store it came from, probably Eaton's, he guesses. But he does remember clearly that every kid was told to choose a gift—anything they wanted, so long as it was under three dollars. They spent hours going over the pictures, thinking about this toy, then comparing it to another one on a different page, then going back to the first one. And of course the price of the one you really wanted was $3.50 and you had to forget it. And then other kids would pull the catalogue away because they said you had it long enough. But you didn't really have it long enough, because you still had not decided.

Each kid got only one present a year. There was nothing on their birthdays, nothing if they were sick and stuck in bed, just one toy once a year on a day called Christmas.

But Don didn't talk about it with bitterness. He said that because they got only one, it was precious. And then months would go by, months of doing schoolwork and lining up for dinner and standing by their beds on Sundays and they would forget about the pictures in the catalogue, or they would try to forget.

As Christmas drew near there were no decorations, no tree and no music. But on Christmas Eve they were told to go to bed early. They pretended they were sleeping, but through their squinched eyelids they could see the housemother walking down the aisles between the beds, tying a stocking on the foot of each one. The stockings were made from the red mesh bags that oranges come in.

On Christmas morning they were up early, and every kid in every dorm crawled down to the end of their beds, grabbing at the stockings. At the top of every one was a half pound of dates. "We didn't like them," said Don. "They were sticky and it was hard to get our hands past them. Next in every stocking was an orange, to keep the children healthy, the orphanage officials said.

"But past the orange, we could feel the rustle of the paper. We could just reach it with our fingertips," he said. "That was everything."

Now, more than fifty years later, he said he could still remember tearing open that paper. He couldn't remember what was inside; the toy is forgotten. But to open it, to open a present just for him, that was the real gift.

Since then, Don has had children and grandchildren

119

and he has watched countless presents being opened on Christmas mornings. There are always decorations and a tree and music. But it is the sound of paper being torn by tiny fingers that puts a smile on his face, and sometimes tears in his eyes.

GRANNY

My granny was hard to believe. There was nothing she could not do. She died when my mother was five years old, and I never met the granny on the other side of the family. On paper that leaves me without a grandmother. But later, when I learned about her, she turned out to be the most wonderful, courageous woman in the world.

My kids, who had two grandmothers, asked me whether I felt left out because I never had anyone to call Granny. Nope, I told them, many people never knew their grandparents, and you can't miss what you never had. Then one day my daughter Colleen and I were in the gift shop of the art gallery and she found a black-and-white photo of a woman sitting on the back seat of a motorcycle. This grey-haired, maybe English, maybe German woman wore a long cloth overcoat and a cloth hat. She had a look on her face that said somebody was late and somebody was going to get a piece of her mind when he got back.

"Why don't you make her your grandmother?" my daughter asked. Then she would have a great-grandmother, she pointed out. Presto, that was all it took—a good idea and a photo, and I had an ancestor. Many people have old photos of stern-faced grandparents on their walls with no unique characteristics. We had one that rode on the back of a motorcycle.

"I bet she is waiting for Granddad," Colleen said, "and he is taking a long time to say goodbye to his friends." And there began the stories. Simple ones at first, like Granny never rode in that sidecar that was attached to the motorcycle. No sir, she liked sitting up right behind Grandpa, even if her coat straddled the back fender. And she always carried the umbrella that was in her hand in the photo, and when it rained, my son Sean said, "She would tell Grandpa to slow down and she would tilt the umbrella over their heads and hold it into the wind and they would ride out the storm."

Over the years we came up with many stories about Grandma and that motorcycle, and in time the stories became true. When she saw someone hitchhiking, especially if they looked tired, she would tell them to get into the sidecar and she would make Grandpa drive them to wherever they were going, even if it was in the opposite direction from where Gramps and Grandma were headed.

There was the time when Grandpa was very sick and needed a doctor. They didn't have a telephone and Grandma had to fetch the doctor in town, but she had never driven the motorcycle herself. This, Sean reminded me, was during the war.

"And she didn't even know how to start the motor," Colleen said. "But she knew if Granddad could drive it, so could she."

"There was nothing she couldn't do," said Sean.

She pushed on the pedal and the motorcycle started, and it took her a few shaky miles but she finally got control of it. She was bouncing along country roads when she ran into an army convoy. This was the best part of the story, my kids said. She didn't know whether they were friend or foe so she got out a white handkerchief and her little case of precious rouge that she always carried, and she painted a red cross on the white flag. Then she tied the flag to her umbrella and stuck it out of the sidecar, and she barrelled right down the middle of that convoy. No one stopped her.

She got to town and picked up the doctor and brought him back, and Grandpa was saved. Grandma was wonderful.

In time the truth came out. We did not adopt her, she adopted us. But being adopted is better than having matching genes because genes only make you look like someone. Being chosen makes you want to be like them, and we wanted to be like Grandma.

What we inherited from her—or at least what I hope we inherited—is some of the defiance I see in her face as she sits on the seat of that motorcycle. She is one tough woman. That's my grandma. You don't mess with her. The more I look at her picture, the more she seems to tell me.

And whenever my kids tell their friends about their great grandmother, they have an unblinking audience. "Wow, you're lucky," their friends say. My kids just smile, and say that Grandma was so wonderful it is hard to believe.

CRASH LANDING

I was on an airplane recently and I got the urge to write a letter. The urge came after I saw a fellow sitting across the aisle reading a magazine about flying, and I wanted to write to Eddie Huggins, the best pilot I ever knew. I didn't have a computer or any writing paper with me, so I wrote on an air sickness bag.

When we were small, we all wanted to join the air force and fly fighter jets. We wanted this because Eddie took off into the sky and sailed just about anywhere he wanted. Eddie was the same age as us, but he was short and fat and he couldn't get off the ground when the rest of us were climbing fences and telephone poles. Then one day he learned to make paper airplanes, and suddenly it was as though he was able to go as high as the moon.

He could make planes that flew in loops and others that settled down on just about any spot that you could name. He learned a lot about real planes too, but his real talent was to design squadrons of different planes with nothing but paper.

As I wrote to him, I remembered how he had tried to

teach us to fold the paper. Most of us wound up with planes that had one wing up and one down and they crashed on takeoff, but it wasn't because he was a bad teacher. Eddie set up the equivalent of a pilot training school. He understood the mysteries of thrust and drag, although he had no idea what those words meant. And he had that special something, that knack that separates the really great pilots from those who merely drive an airplane. It must have been the way he folded the paper and the spot where he placed his fingers and the angle at which he threw it, because when Eddie let go of that page torn from a notebook it flew farther and higher than any of us could believe.

Then came the terrible day when someone hit Miss Johnson in the back of the head with a paper airplane. Miss Johnson was the teacher who had tried to murder the celery, and although she was kind and patient, hitting her in the head with an airplane was not allowed.

"Eddie!" She yelled out his name before she turned around. "Eddie, come up here."

"It wasn't me," he said from the back of the class.

Miss Johnson knew every kid in the class. She knew that Eddie drew pictures of airplanes on his homework. She knew that he was the only kid in class who knew what he wanted to do when he grew up. Therefore, she knew that he was guilty.

"Is this your idea of a joke?" she said to him.

"No, ma'am," he said. He looked at the airplane. "That's not my design."

"Well, you go straight to the principal and explain that to her."

Luckily, Mrs. Flag, the principal, was a wise woman. Eddie spent an hour with her, showing her how the offending plane could only go about ten feet, while an aircraft of his design would circle inside her office, passing by all four walls. By the end of the afternoon Eddie was teaching Mrs. Flag how to make airplanes that she could throw from her desk and that would land on her bookcase on the other side of the room.

I finished the letter and thanked him for the good times we had in Eddie's Flying School. Then I added a PS: "Remember that airplane that hit Miss Johnson? It's time I confessed. I didn't mean to hit her, but I threw it. I tried to confess, but I didn't talk loud enough for Miss Johnson to hear."

A week later I got a letter back. Inside was a drawing of a short, fat pilot. The note said: "Bag received. Your flying is improving. Bag was empty. And don't worry about the crash landing back in school. We all survived."

Eddie never made it into a real cockpit. He was too short and too fat and his glasses were too thick for him to get into the military. He became a social worker and spent much of his time in low-income neighbourhoods, where he taught a whole bunch of really poor kids how to make paper airplanes. Several of those kids wound up in the air force, putting jet planes up on top of the clouds.

The Gutter Navy

My friend Johnny Martin planned on being a sailor when he grew up, because his big brother was in the Navy. What Johnny turned out to be was an admiral in the gutter fleet.

Every kid everywhere in the world who is lucky enough to have a curb and a street and a rainstorm has served on a ship in that narrow ocean. You don't need anything but a Popsicle stick, or leaves or paper or wooden matches, and you can set sail at high speed down the street and rescue your ship just before it plunges into the sewer. You run alongside it, watching it navigate around car tires and bounce over rapids made of dirt and broken glass. It is exciting and it gives you something to do while you get soaked in the rain.

Johnny sailed every time there was a storm, and it takes a good storm to make enough rain to get the boats really moving. He sailed ice cream sticks, and sometimes he cut points in one end to make bows, and sometimes he tied two or three sticks together to make a battleship. Sometimes he had a convoy going down the gutter.

But there came the day when a shoe came out of nowhere and kicked his boat flat against the curb. Johnny looked up and saw a kid who was one of those humans born with a thorn in his soul. His name was Stan and he lived way down at the end of the block and he loved breaking things. He was bigger than Johnny.

"You're going to pay for that," said Johnny.

Kids in this neighbourhood did not respond to acts of aggression with statements like, "Why did you do that?" or "That's not nice," or "I'm going to tell your mother." Nope. It was "You're going to pay," and that was despite Johnny being six inches shorter and two years younger than his enemy.

Stan said he was going to sail his boats in that spot and Johnny should get lost. He pushed Johnny out of the way, took out his own sticks and started sailing, and Johnny disappeared. But as you may guess, Johnny did not go home. He went half a block away and crouched in front of a parked car, where he rapidly piled up stones, sticks and scraps of newspaper to divert the urban river right out into the bus lane.

He slipped away just before Stan's boats came by. Stan was ten feet behind, trying to keep up with his fleet, and he did not see the water turning because Johnny had hidden his aqueduct behind a car tire. Just as Stan was about to catch up with his boats they made a sharp left turn, and before he could grab them they were shooting out into the street and disappearing under big crushing tires.

"That's how the Navy sinks the enemy," said Johnny. "My brother taught me that."

Most people who build model ships secretly pretend their boats go into battle. They picture cannons firing and sailors clenching sabres in their teeth. They all have some of Johnny's spirit in them. But Johnny actually engaged the enemy, and in the battle of the gutter he raised the flag of victory.

First Kiss

I am going to tell you why Bill didn't become an actor. Bill makes his living with a camera. He and I were standing outside a school, watching some little kids go inside to perform a Christmas play because we were going to do a story about them, when Bill told me it was something like that that had changed his life.

Bill was nine years old, in grade four, and there was a girl. The U-turns in a guy's life are almost always caused by girls. Her name was Sheryl Vogel, and she had won the heart of Bill, but as often happens in love stories, she didn't know it.

First love is a game that everyone plays but no one knows the rules. He wanted her to notice him, so he left things on her desk, little things like unsigned notes saying, "I love you." Then he would try to watch her as she read the note. But he only watched her out of the corner of an eye. He did not move his head. He did not smile or point to himself or anything. In fact, he was trembling at the thought that she might notice him. Insanity is one of the problems with first love. Sheryl would put the notes away and go back to her schoolwork, something Bill could not think about at all.

In the hallway he would try to bump into her accidentally, but all she said was, "Hey, watch where you're going."

Then, halfway into the school year, Bill got his big chance. Their class was putting on a play and Sheryl was in it. So Bill said he wanted to be an actor.

There was not much rehearsing; they only had small parts. Sheryl was playing the girl in a carnival sideshow who was running a kissing booth, and Bill's job was to stand in line and give her a kiss.

"You don't really have to touch," the teacher told them.

Bill heard nothing. He was in heaven.

"But Bill," said the teacher, "the most important thing is right after you pretend to kiss Sheryl, you say as loud as you can, 'On with the show'."

The sun was down when the curtain went up. What a perfect night for love. The air buzzed with excitement.

The audience was in their seats, the stage was crowded with actors. Then it was time for Bill's starring moment. He stepped out from the line of boys in front of the kissing booth, his heart pounding. He leaned over and, with his lips protruding and tight as spandex, he made full contact with Sheryl's lips. And there he stayed. And stayed.

"Say something," Sheryl whispered.

But Bill said nothing. Everyone on stage walked in circles waiting for the cue words. Then they walked some more. But no one said, "On with the show."

"Say it," insisted Sheryl, moving her lips against his, this time with more urgency.

But Bill was in bliss. There was no play, no script, no audience. All he knew was that he was kissing Sheryl, and he was in love and she must be too, even if she kept trying to talk while they were doing it.

Then from behind him he heard, "On with the show." It was his teacher's voice. Suddenly—whoops—it all came back. He stood up and shouted, "On with the show," then he bent down for another kiss.

The audience loved it. He remembers the laughter. He also remembers what Sheryl said as his lips reached out for a second time. She stood up and shouted, "Next!" It was the last word he ever heard her say.

Older folks with TV soap operas and weddings and divorce courts sometimes forget how early we get on the potholed road of love. Grownups call it cute, but those first flickers of a dewy soft heart often set us in directions we keep to until our skin is wrinkled.

A year or so after the school play, Bill noticed Lucy. Lucy did not last long either. He just remembers that he looked at her, and that he was breathing deeply when he followed her into the camera club.

That was forty years ago. After he told his story, Bill picked up his camera and we went off to see the children's Christmas play, which looked fine to us. The only thing we couldn't see were the hearts that were pounding on that stage, and the stories that were not in the script.

A Little Art

One warm day a few years ago, there was a knock on my door. It was my little neighbour Jamie, who was six and wanted to earn some extra cash for summer. The market for lemonade stands was saturated, and empty pop cans were hard to find with everyone drinking bottled water, but she had a brilliant idea.

She got the idea after her parents had come back from an art and framing shop with a new picture for their wall. It showed a sunset with trees and houses. "I can't believe how much they charged for it," her father said. Jamie thought about it and suddenly her future was clear. She was already an artist. She was good at face painting and making chalk drawings on the sidewalk. And now she had the secret for cashing in on lines and squiggles. Spread your art around.

"Hello," I said to her as she stood at my door.

"I have a picture I drew of your house," she said.

She pointed to the paper. on which were drawn four lines, a rectangle, with a triangle on top. "That's where you live," she said. "And there is you, standing in front of it. And there is your cat." There was a stick man that was clearly me, standing in front of my house, and some ovals and other lines that showed my cat. The drawing was very lifelike—she even had ears. "You can buy it for two dollars," Jamie said. The price was written at the top.

"Well, two dollars is a lot," I said. "How about twenty-five cents?"

"OK."

I stuck the picture on the refrigerator with a magnet and admired it because I had never had a customized, personalized house portrait before. But I only recognized the artist's genius when I talked to another neighbour. She too had a picture of her house, showing herself and her dog. It was the same picture I had, except the tabby had become a collie. And her neighbour on the other side also had a picture drawn in the same motif.

"But you don't have a cat or a dog," I said to him.

He told me that Jamie had explained to him that the cat portrayed belonged to his neighbour, but that it sometimes walked across his front yard, so she drew it and made a sale. He also mentioned that he had paid the whole two dollars, meaning Jamie's art was already increasing in value.

Later I saw Jamie standing in front of a house way down at the end of the block. She was drawing four lines with a triangle on top and circles and lines that became a person and a cat.

"Suppose they have a bird?" I asked.

"That's inside the house," she said. "You can't see it."

If you have invested in one of Jamie's early works, I suggest that you frame it. In fifty years the Vancouver Art Gallery may be showing them, and charging a lot more than two dollars just to have a look at the genius of youth.

Blowing Out the Candles

You will see them this weekend adding to the traffic crush. On Saturday and Sunday they will be driving back and forth across town as they do every weekend, with a desperation that was unknown only a few years ago. In each car: one adult and one child, going to a birthday party.

Once upon a time, when the world was simpler, a child's birthday was observed with a cake and a small family gathering. Now the birthday party is an inescapable step in social development. Parents with five- and six-year-olds get invitations from at least half the kids in the daycare or kindergarten class and nearly all of their neighbours. None of them can be turned down.

"Not go??!! You don't want me to go to Jimmy's party?! Mommy! He's my best friend!"

As a result, parents chauffeur their kids at least twice a month to the birthday bashes of kids they could not recognize if they were staring at their mug shots. The numbers go up in May, which seems to be the month of choice to be born. In May you go to a party every week. Over a year you average two a month, unless you have two children. Then it is four parties a month. That's forty-eight parties a year.

And they all take place on weekends, which is the only time to have a children's birthday party because the children are too busy during the week with sports and piano. Weekends fit in with the children's schedule, but not necessarily yours. Just when you would rather go shopping or play golf or wash the car or simply bang your head against the wall, no. There is a party waiting.

"Another party? No. Not two! No, don't tell me there are two parties on the same day!"

"But," says cute little Shannon, looking up at her mother with her six-year-old innocent face, "it's easy, Mommy. One party is in the morning and the other in the afternoon. I don't have to miss either one."

And so Shannon and her mother leave home two hours before the first party so they can buy presents for birthday children. Then they sit in the car a block away from the first party while Shannon's mother wraps the first present. She drives to the party house and out skips Shannon. Mother then rushes to the grocery store, shops, drives back to the first party and sits in the car outside, wrapping the gift for the second party.

Shannon bounces out of the first party wired on ice cream and sugar-frosted cake. "Mommy, Mommy, let's go quick. The other party's already started." A social calendar jet-setter barely out of the child safety seat.

And nothing, nothing is allowed to stop a child on his or her way to a party. Take the case of Peter, who was going to drive his five-year-old son Mason to a party in Burnaby. Peter's car wouldn't start.

"Oh, no!" That was from Mason, not his father, and it meant: "Do something fast, Dad, before I have a panic attack."

Peter called BCAA. They would be there in twenty minutes. No problem, Peter told his son, they would just be a little late for the party. But when the nice BCAA man arrived, he told Peter that his starter motor was worn out. And BCAA doesn't fix starter motors. Big problem.

Peter called a taxi. But it was raining, and taxis are busy when it rains. It would be a thirty-minute wait. The bus would be quicker, Peter decided. They ran to the corner, Peter holding the present with one hand and Mason with the other, and got to the bus stop just in time to see the bus they wanted getting smaller as it drove away.

They ran to the SkyTrain station—in the rain, without an umbrella. When they disembarked, they were still seven blocks away from their destination. And it was raining harder.

By the time they got to the party they were soaked, and they were so late that there were only a few stragglers left and all the food was gone. Half an hour later, Peter and Mason were the last to leave. Peter's clothes were still wet, he was exhausted and hungry, and he felt that he had let his son down.

"Gee," said Mason to his father on the way out, "that was fun. That was the best ever."

Dying

Everyone does it, eventually. We were sitting at the breakfast table when I asked my mother-in-law to tell me something happy that had happened to her when she was little. I like happy stories. She thought for a moment, going back over a childhood that for an instant became only yesterday, and she said, "Funerals. I like funerals."

"You're kidding," I said.

"No, honest. They were the best times."

My mother-in-law is from the West Indies and her memories have nothing to do with the travel brochures that show sun and sand and palm trees. Her life was like most in a struggling nation. You worried about food and the future. Until someone died. "And then there was a big party," she said.

The men made the casket and the women sewed the cloth to be wrapped around the body. This was before the great family event of death was physically sanitized and emotionally sterilized by funeral homes. "The little girls picked the flowers, wildflowers," she said. There were no florists. You did not call up and order a wreath and charge it to your credit card and never see it until you went to the funeral.

The people of the village, "and I mean all the people," she said, brought food and rum and they smoked and drank and everyone ate. The body lay in the house and everyone stood around it telling stories about the person and crying and laughing. No one was afraid of the body, not even the kids.

"Funerals now," she said, shaking her head over a practice that does not seem real to her, "are so depressing, even the dead must get spooked."

She said that when her godmother died she had the privilege of washing her feet. She was six years old. The older girls and women cleaned the rest of the body. Can you imagine a six-year-old, or a twenty-six-year-old, who would do that now? Death is too scary for us. We hire people to wash and dress and put makeup on those whom we once loved and cherished.

"Then the men would dig the grave," she said. "But we had to give them rum." They were not unionized grave-diggers. They were not paid. They were neighbours, and they drank while they dug. "And sometimes they drank so much," she said, and now her eyes were laughing with the memory, "they would fall down in the bottom of the grave and we would have to get other men to pull them out so we could lower the coffin."

The body was always buried on the third day, and that's when the religious men would come. The West Indies had been settled by people of many backgrounds and religions—Christian, Eastern, African, Hindu, Jewish—and sometimes they overlapped.

But the celebration went on for nine days and nine nights. "That's why we call it Nine Night, no matter what the religion," she said.

On the last night was the biggest party. There was more food and rum and singing and music, and sometimes drums, and always dominoes. "Maybe that's why we didn't suffer with the sadness."

She said she used to look forward to funerals. Even if you didn't know the people very well, you still went to eat and sing. She didn't remember any weddings, she said, but she remembered a lot of funerals.

CHRISTMAS MOURNINGS

There are stages of Christmas mornings, my friend John was telling me. Every child goes through them and they recur in a great cycle. It starts at your child's first Christmas. You have to wake her, as he did his little girl, Julie. He and his wife Pat saw the twinkle of Christmas tree lights in Julie's baby eyes.

By the time she was two she knew something big was happening. There was a tree inside the house and she was told that a big, friendly stranger would come in the night and leave her gifts. She was up by seven and she woke her new baby sister, Melany. John and Pat heard the kids moving toward the presents and got up to share the excitement.

By the time Julie was four, she knew what Christmas was all about: lots of gifts and lots of fun, and the earlier you get to them, the more fun you have. She was up at six and woke Melany and their new baby sister, Christa. John and Pat heard them heading toward the presents and dragged themselves out of bed.

The next year Julie and Melany and Christa were up at five.

"Go back to bed," their parents said.

"But we want to see what Santa brought!"

John and Pat felt unsteady on their feet. They had been up wrapping those presents until 2:00 a.m. They tried to smile.

And so it continued through the years. As the girls grew older, they got up earlier and earlier, trying to catch a glimpse of Santa. Each year they missed him—the gifts were already there when they woke up. But since they were up, they might as well stay up. And naturally they did not want their parents to miss out on the fun, so they woke them up too, at 4:15 in the morning.

"Noooo," moaned their father.

"Go back to bed," pleaded their mother.

"But Santa's been here!" their daughters said all at once. "Come and see!"

What Pat and John could see were lights flicking on in a few other homes. They were not alone. As the years passed, the trend continued. Seven- and eight-year-olds can get by on incredibly little sleep on the night before Christmas. And since they had two more daughters who would grow to age seven and eight, John and Pat could look forward to many more years of enjoying the thrill of Christmas morning in the middle of the night.

Eventually, John was happy to tell me, they reached another stage, and things got very different. While all around them the windows of the homes where little children lived were glowing hours before the sun came up, John and Pat were still asleep. They awoke when they were rested. They said Merry Christmas to each other. They made coffee and they gazed at the tree.

Their little darlings had become teenagers, and just as when they were babies, their parents had to go into their bedrooms and say, "Wake up, it's Christmas morning!"

And the teenagers moaned, "Noooo, it's too early."

PS. Two years after John told me this story his youngest daughter Christa, nineteen years old, was killed in a car crash. Christmas is different now. The great moments that we are given are the only truly precious gifts we ever get.

Burning Ashes

Dying can be hard. Especially when the dying starts when you are a teenager and ends fifty years later, and the killers are advertising and fashion.

My mother had lung cancer. She died painfully and slowly. She was still alive when I got to the hospital because she was on life support—a breathing machine, wires, tubes, all inserted into her limp body, and every time the machine forced a measured amount of air through the tube and into her lungs, her whole body jerked on the bed.

She was unconscious. They told me she was brain dead. I whispered in her ear and a tear came out of her eye, and one of the machines said that said her heart rate went up, if only for a moment.

She had left instructions to me and to everyone that she was not to be kept alive by machines. I signed the papers, and they unplugged her. But she did not die right away. It is something in nature, I suppose, that makes a living creature try to hold on, no matter what. The doctors said it was her brain stem automatically keeping her diaphragm going, but every breath was a gargantuan struggle to pull air into lungs that were useless. She was breathing like a person with asthma climbing a mountain. We wished she would die.

A few years earlier her chest had been cut open and half of one of her cancerous lungs was removed. I had helped her check into the hospital, and she had insisted on going outside for one more cigarette before getting into her hospital gown. A year later she had an identical operation, and a lobe was taken off her other lung.

She had started smoking when she was a teenager. No one told her it was bad for her health, and even if they had, she would not have listened. Smoking was glamorous. It was beautiful. Exciting men and women did it.

We sat by her bed for four days, four eternally long days after the life support machine was turned off. Four days of watching every breath sweated and strained for before she died. After that, we went through boxes of her old photographs. She was young and happy and she had a cigarette in her hand in almost every photo. At the beach she was smoking. At family gatherings she was smoking. Everyone was smoking. The few who didn't smoke were oddities. "He probably doesn't drink, either." The implication was that he was a wimp.

My mother's burial was fantastic. She wasn't religious and she wanted no service or memorial, but she loved shopping. She did not own much, but she adored going through high-end department stores, looking, touching, comparing. When she found something she deeply wanted, a blouse usually, she would wait and wait until it went on sale. If it was sold out or she missed the sale, she would shrug and let it go. It was a small gamble, and it put some excitement in her life, and she would fancy something else before long.

When she died, my kids were both living in New York and my daughter came up with a list of the best stores in the city. After the cremation we each took some of the ashes in our hands and went into Bonwit Teller and Saks Fifth Avenue and Lord and Taylor, and we spread Grandmother where she most loved to be. She was secretly put to rest in front of the counter where the blouses were sold. She was inconspicuously spread in the shoe department. Then her grandson went into Tiffany's, a jewellery store much too expensive for my mother ever to set foot into. And while the security guards were looking at him, because he is not the type to shop in Tiffany's, his hands were by his sides sprinkling Grandma in front of the diamond counter.

We scattered the remaining ashes from the back of a ferry. They blew out over the water, then settled down for a trip around the world. We liked that. She would have liked that. When we got off the ferry a bus passed by, and on the side was a big ad that pictured a glamorous young woman with a cigarette in her hand. The woman looked a lot like my mother when she was younger: same smile, same joy of living, same cigarette, and possibly the same future.

The Unfinished Story

There is living and there is dying, and everyone, regardless of race, religion or nationality, eventually can show membership in both clubs. But for some there is a splinter group, which no one joins willingly. Once you are drafted into it, you quickly learn to curse everything. It is almost dying, and almost not living. When you see someone like this you wonder what you would do if you were among the chosen, and you say no, please God, no. Shoot me first.

My niece belongs to this club. Her name is Ashley Lauren Fisher, but she likes Ashley Lauren better because it sounds more like a model's name, and she was going to be a model. She is tall, blonde and beautiful. She was also a dancer, a lacrosse coach and a lifeguard. She was a no-fooling-around twenty-three-year-old chick with a jeep and a ponytail.

Then one day at a beach in New Jersey, she dove off a friend's shoulders into an oncoming wave as she had done hundreds of times before, only this time something went terribly wrong. It may have been the angle at which she hit the water, it may have been an extra strong wave. Whatever it was, her head twisted and in that swirling tide she heard a bang in the back of her neck. A bang, that is the way she described it, and that was the end of one life and the beginning of something that is hard to describe.

Suddenly her body was lifeless, paralyzed, dead. She could not move her arms, her hands, her legs, nothing. Her neck was broken. Water rushed over her face and poured into her mouth and lungs. The undertow of foam and surf rolled her over and over, pulling and wrenching whatever might have remained of the spinal cord at the back of her neck. It happened in moments. Her friend pulled her out while more waves pounded on them.

The next chapter of the story was a massive operation in which doctors replaced the shattered bones in her neck with steel rods. But her spinal cord was crushed beyond repair and beyond hope. She could not breathe. A machine pumped air through a tube that went through a hole cut in her throat.

Because of that machine, she could not talk. She could only mouth words. Not even the air of a whisper was there, only lips trying to form silent words, and when you are standing over a bed with someone you love lying on it, and she is filled with tubes and wires, and you cannot understand what she is saying and she cannot make herself be understood, it is a painful thing for both of you.

"What did you say? What did she say? Did you say 'it hurts'? I know it hurts."

More words: "Scared? Yes. We are scared too."

And more: "We don't know. The doctors can't say. But . . . but . . . you've got to believe."

And then her eyes closed and her mother and father and

148

brother's eyes wept. She was in the intensive care unit for twenty-nine days, her mind absolutely clear, her body just lying there. Her friends and family stood around her, massaging her arms and legs, trying to keep the muscles alive, but she could not feel us doing it. We tried to be positive, because that is the only medicine we had, but there were also many shaking heads, and clenched fists, and silent prayers said with wet eyes clamped shut.

But each day when the doctors checked her, she would wink at them and smile. She never once whispered "Why me?" I do not know where she got the courage. It broke my heart in admiration. Because of one wave in the ocean, she cannot brush her teeth or comb her hair or feed herself or scratch an itch on her nose. But she kept mouthing the words, "I am trying."

Night and day family and friends stood by her side, talking to her, whispering encouraging words and massaging her legs and arms, hoping some nerves somewhere would wake up. She screwed up her face and tried with all her heart and strength to move her fingers. We raised her arm so that she could see her hand. She stared at the fingers. They did not move.

We tried to understand what she was saying. I have more sympathy for the deaf now. Lip reading is hard. So many words can be confused with other words, meanings are lost and hopelessness is all you hear.

On the twenty-third day the doctors took her off the breathing machine just for a few minutes to see if she could live on her own. The hole in her throat was closed with a bandage, and this would be a good day because she would be able to speak again, even if just a few words.

The nurses warned Ashley and us that because she had not talked for more than three weeks, her words would sound funny and they would come slowly. We were ready. But what would be the first thing she would try to say? Would it be bitterness or determination, or love or fatalism? We stood around the bed, leaning close. She spoke very slowly, and her first words were, and I am quoting her exactly: "I wish some of you would not eat so much garlic before you come to visit me."

The room in the trauma centre exploded with laughter. The tension of a month of unbearable heaviness had been broken by a girl—a woman—who is paralyzed in her body, but not in her spirit. We ate mints, and she laughed.

The doctors told her that the future does not look good. The paralysis is total. But they did not count on the spirit that tries to make that body move, the spirit that makes others laugh in the face of tears. That spirit cannot be paralyzed.

Some weeks later, when Valerie and I told Ashley that we had to fly home and go back to work, she told me her story was just beginning. "It will end when I can walk," she said.

That is why this story is unfinished. I give you only the beginning and middle of it. We are waiting for that ending because any girl who can wink after her neck is broken is not going to quit until she can play the piano again and run through a field of wildflowers. That is the only ending that belongs here, and when that happens this story will be finished, no matter how long we have to wait.

Over the next two years Ashley tried to kill herself,

which is not easy to do when you cannot move. And she went into great, deep despair, which is normal for someone who cannot move. Death would be better, she said.

She wrote to me on a special computer, "I hate being a gimp. That's what it is, a painful way to survive. Torture. Will I be fixed someday?"

But then this woman, who had disdained reading and who preferred sports and dating and snowboarding before her accident, began writing poetry. Two years after her accident:

Bluegrass and lemonade—
dirty feet and guitars—
holding hands on pink and periwinkle linen—
daytime dreaming while sipping
on fusions and forgetting foreverness.

And she began changing the only thing she could change: her mind. In a message in the dead of winter, she wrote: "I was outside and decided I would sing. Sing anything that came to mind. I know all the cold birds that usually sing to me would find it soothing. So, I sang with gusto, but kept the harmony soft."

On her birthday, after four years of sitting down, she planned a vacation at a resort near the ocean. "It's my first real vacation," she wrote before she left. "I'm stoked. The sun. The cute gay men. The experience of travel. The shopping. And will I? Will I see the beach? Will I cry? Will I be brave? Will I ever be fixed?"

We all go through hell sometime. We all face the corrupt judge sometime. We all lose almost everything sometime. Some of us make it to the other end.

151

Two weeks later she wrote: "I saw the beach and sat by the pool. I ate grilled fish and drank Ashley Browns, a drink named after Bobbi Brown and I."

And then she added: "Too many men, too little time."

You can almost taste it, you can almost feel it in the air, see it in the words and sense it in the smile. It may not come quickly, but the story will have an ending, and it will be a good one.

Toys Were Us

Once upon a time, two-wheeled bicycles had only one gear. We are talking about an era just a few hours after the ice age. You went faster by pedalling harder. And the fastest one on a bike was the one who pedalled the hardest and had the most to prove, not the one with the best gears. But that is another story from an old neighbourhood elsewhere in this book.

That was also a time when we had roller skates made out of metal. The trouble was, we didn't have many of them because they rusted so easily. They would rust if they were left out in the rain or went through a puddle, and they were always being left out in the rain or going through puddles. You had to have a key to tighten these skates onto your shoes. And that key, well, we were always losing it. After a while, what most kids were left with was one rusty skate with wheels that would not turn, and no key.

Johnny Martin hungered for things like that. He could make magic out of anything he could get his hands on. Even when he was ten or twelve he would get scraps of wood and build a fort in the concrete backyard between the row houses.

I don't know how he got a hammer or nails or how he learned how to use them. He got no instruction at home. His father was always in the bar and his mother was always working. But somehow he taught himself to cut and nail, and he would turn junk wood into one-room homes with windows and doors. They were strong enough for us to stand on and big enough for three or four of us to crawl into and with our knees pulled close to our chests, we could escape from the outside.

Johnny loved skates too. Broken, rusted, lost skates. He would take them apart and hammer them onto the ends of a two-by-four. Then he would nail a wooden crate on the front and a broken broomstick to the crate as handlebars, for steering. He would get some oil by crawling under cars parked on the street and rubbing his hands under the crankcases, then wipe the residue from his fingers onto the rusty skate wheels.

Then, magically, he had a scooter, and we would all try to climb on it. Everyone would take a ride, and in half an hour it was smashed. The skates were pulled loose when we hit potholes and the crate was demolished when we hit walls. But this did not bother Johnny. He did not sit down and groan or complain. He built things to use, and a couple of weeks later he would find another skate and make another scooter.

This was thirty years before some people made millions off skateboards. But Johnny knew nothing of plastic, and the term *recycling* would not become a household word for years. He only knew that if you had something old and broken, and you put some work into it, you could turn it into something to use.

I don't know where Johnny is now, or even if he is still alive. But if he is, I bet he has a bunch of kids hanging around his garage, where he is fixing things. That would make a second generation of kids who believed that he could work magic. Real magic. Not magic with tricks, but the kind of magic that can make a dead toy come alive again. It is a magic that is almost gone from our world.

These thoughts came to me recently when I was in a second-hand store and saw a rusty, solitary skate. I paid five dollars for it and brought it home with great pride. I put it down in front of my wife.

"I could have brought you flowers," I said, "but just look at this beauty."

"Not another piece of junk," she sighed.

"But I can make a scooter and give it to a neighbour-hood kid," I replied.

"They all have ten-speed mountain bikes," she said, "and two-hundred-dollar skateboards."

She was right. We do not rebuild, we refinance so that we can reorder a state-of-the-art replacement.

"I bet Johnny would know what to do with it," I said.

"Yes," said my wife in her insightful way, "Johnny was a genius at keeping things alive."

I nodded, while trying to turn the rusted wheels that would not turn.

"So," she continued, "he would have bought the flowers."

THE PERFECT GARDEN

The best garden I ever saw was over the fence behind the armory on Beatty Street in Vancouver. It was at the bottom of a steep incline almost too hard to climb. By 2002 it was filled with garbage that had been thrown over the fence. But in 1985 I looked through that same fence, and hidden at the bottom of the slope, through brambles and weeds, I saw something glittering, something moving and reflecting the sun.

I found an opening in the fence and climbed through it, and holding on tightly and still slipping on the loose dirt, I got to the bottom. There I found a level pathway made of planks of wood. I had to crouch to walk on the wood because the blackberries were thick overhead. The planks led to an opening in the brambles not visible from above.

There were rows of tulips cut from plastic plates and duct-taped to sticks. There was a patch of Popsicle sticks with a ribbon tied to the top of each, and they were surrounded by pieces of a broken mirror so that as you looked down you could see both sides of the patch at once. Another piece of mirror lay on the ground surrounded by stones, making a pond. Ribbons and plastic sunflowers hung in the lower branches of the scrabble trees.

I was there for only a few minutes before an ancient, bone-thin man with white hair and a white beard came down the slope.

"You like it?" he asked.

He didn't say, "Hey, what are you doing here?" He didn't say, "Be careful," or "Don't hurt anything," or "Get out of here, this is mine." He asked if I liked his garden. I did a story about him for television. His name was Carl Verronen and he had been a cook in a logging camp. Now that he was old he lived by himself in the Sandman Hotel and tended his garden, which was just a block from the hotel. That was all. That was his story. A week later I went back to visit and he told me he was being evicted because of Expo 86, the world's fair, which was being set up in the area adjacent to his garden.

The designers of the fair said that they wanted the surrounding areas to look as good as possible, which meant that anything that looked out of place would have to go. Expo officials said the garden was nothing, no loss. It was just some plastic plates, not even a real garden.

A few weeks later the garden was ripped apart. Expo came and went and the gardener died and the weeds grew, and now the garden is a decaying dump of litter at the back of an abandoned parking lot. Gardens are like the people who make them: they don't last forever. But for one brief shining moment that patch over the fence was a work of primrose beauty, a garden where imagination flourished and where a gardener made the earth a better place.

War of the Pond

What everyone needs, I was told by a friend, is the sound of water running over rocks and dripping into a pond in their own backyard. It will bring peace, said the friend, who installs beautiful professional ponds.

Peace is what I wanted, but I figured I could build the pond myself and get cut-rate peace. I got a shovel and started digging. The spot I chose was an old zucchini patch that I could live without. Digging was hard work, but I told myself that peace is worth some sweat and dirty hands. I dug, and dug more, and when the sun set behind the pile of dirt I had dug out of the hole, I had trouble seeing. Peace is worth a little darkness, I told myself.

"What are you doing?" said my wife. I couldn't see her, but I could hear her.

"I'm digging so we will have peace," I said over the hill of dirt.

"I didn't know we didn't have peace," she said.

I tossed up a shovel full of dirt.

"Watch it," she said.

I tried to climb out of the hole, but I had made a mistake.

The hole was nearly as deep as I am tall. The bottom was so narrow that I could not move my feet, and the sides sloped up and out so that I could not reach the edges. I had dug a cone-shaped coffee filter and I was the grounds stuck at the bottom.

"Can you help me?" I asked.

"I thought you were finding peace down there," my wife said.

She got down on one knee and reached over, and I grabbed her hand and climbed up on my knees, listening to how I really should go on a diet. I got to the top and looked down at the shovel, which was still at the bottom. And there ended the first night of searching for peace.

The next day I climbed down and got the shovel and dug my way out, making the pond much larger than I wanted. Then I bought a plastic liner and spread it over the hole. But it needed rocks, big rocks, to hold down the edges on the ground. So I drove to a river and hauled up many big stones. It was hard work, but peace is worth it, I told myself. I drove home with the back of the car almost dragging on the ground and me staring up at the sky through the windshield.

Before unloading the car, I went inside and made a lunch of a salami sandwich and potato salad and beer, and put it out on the table just as my wife returned home. You know the look a woman can make, sort of raising one eyebrow and bending the lips down, the look that says, "I caught you, and you and I know that you don't listen to anything I say." She says that part without moving her lips, and then adds, with a mixture of sarcasm and general unpleasantness, "I thought you were on a diet."

"But bringing peace into our yard takes energy," I said.

I took my beer and sandwich and potato salad outside and sat by the edge of the hole. I was too tired to unload the car but it was nice and peaceful just to sit there and imagine how the water would flow and the fish would swim. Then I heard a thump, followed by another thump. My wife was unloading the car. Goodbye sandwich.

"I need to use the car for grocery shopping," she said.

"Now?"

"No, not now," she said. "I'll wait until you help me take these rocks out."

Sometimes on the road to peace you can stub your toe.

I put the rocks on the plastic around the rim of the hole, filled the hole with water and got some fish and plants from the pet store and some chemicals to keep the fish alive and put them all in the water. I looked at it lovingly. Then I went to bed.

Later, while golden fins glided through my dreams, the raccoons called a meeting in my yard. "We can be thankful," they said, "for another man searching for peace." First they rolled the rocks into the water. Then they ripped up the plants. And then they ate the fish.

In the morning I stood by the muddy hole, shaking my fist. "No one is going to steal my peace," I said loud enough to wake the neighbours.

I bought more plants and a second set of fish, the ten-cent-apiece economy-priced ones.

To defend my peace I spread chicken wire across the pond, and to keep the raccoons from lifting it I hammered the edges down with tent pegs. "Don't mess with my peace," I said as I went to bed.

The raccoons did not lift the wire. No, raccoons are too smart to work that hard. They used the wire as a bridge to get to the middle of the pond where they could rip up the plants and eat the fish.

I bought a third set of fish, poor fish. Then I laid a sheet of plywood over the pond. "This is war," I told my wife. "We are defending the right to have a peaceful yard."

The counterattack came after dark. First the plywood defence fell as the raccoons pushed it aside. Then the fish were taken captive and eaten. The next day I put rocks on the plywood. My wife said that it was a very ugly thing I had created. I told her there was a principle involved. We were fighting for peace. More fish went in.

That night the raccoons rolled the rocks away. Then they moved the plywood, which caused them to work up an appetite, so they ate the fish. I came back the next morning with a sledgehammer and drove fence posts into the ground around the pond. Then I wrapped chicken wire around the posts and put another layer of wire across the top. It looked like a prison, but so what? War isn't pretty. I was now a front-line soldier for peace. Then I got more fish. I couldn't even look them in the eye. "You are heroes," I said as I dumped them through the wire and into the water. I didn't sleep that night. Would the defence hold?

In the morning—victory. The raccoons had only been able to push their arms through the holes of the fence, and the fish had survived. However, the rocks around the edge of the pond had not. The raccoons had rolled them into the water, which loosened the plastic liner, which let half the water leak out of the pond.

But half a victory was a start. I took down the fence, pulled the rocks out of the bottom of the pond and put them back on the edge of the plastic, and replaced the fence. Then I put a second fence around the first and slid sheets of plywood between the two fences, making a dark fortress inside. It was true that I couldn't see the fish, but peace cannot be won without sacrifice. What was important was that the structure would keep the raccoons out. I would win. I would be victorious. Soon I could enjoy my fish in peace.

"Would you please get that out of the garden," said my wife. "It looks like an outhouse."

"I can't," I said, "it's my place of peace."

"If you want any peace, you will make it disappear," she said.

That is why I once again have a zucchini patch, right where the fish pond was. It is very peaceful watching the zucchinis grow. And for additional entertainment I can look up and watch the activities of my neighbour, who has decided to search for peace by building a pond in his backyard.

THE PORTABLE BACKYARD

When we were ten years old we heard a story in school about country kids. I have forgotten the story, but I remember the drawing on the cover of the book. It showed two boys sitting by a stream holding fishing poles. The other kids and I did not care about the stream or the fish or the gear. We did not care about the tree they were leaning against. What we wanted were those pieces of straw that the boys held in their mouths like drooping foot-long toothpicks.

"Where can you get those?" asked Tommy, who possibly had never set foot on a patch of grass in his life.

"You can probably buy them at the five-and-dime," said Vinnie, who had never climbed a tree or sniffed a flower.

"If we knew where to steal them we could do that," said Johnny. "And we wouldn't get into trouble because there can't be a law against stealing straw."

We spent that afternoon going to every store in the neighbourhood, and we got chased out of most and laughed out of a few. Finally we gave up and went back to toothpicks.

Around the same time I saw an ad in a comic book: "Grow Your Own Backyard Indoors." There was a drawing of a man mowing a grass-covered yard. In one corner was a picnic table and in another was a doghouse with a dog sticking its head out. "Brighten up your apartment with your own 12"x 8" grass yard."

That is for me! I am sending this coupon in right now, with—a dollar. A what? A dollar?! That was an hour's wage for a secretary. A dollar was hard to come by, and even harder to part with. I hunted through all my hiding places and came up with forty cents. I found some bottles by the garbage, two cents deposit each. I found an unopened pack of my mother's cigarettes. If you bought them in a machine, as she did sometimes, you got back two cents change under the cellophane after you put a quarter into the machine. She would forgive me when I told her we would have a garden to walk in.

I measured out twelve feet by eight feet in the kitchen. Wow, that was big. We would have to put the kitchen table on the lawn. My mother would love that. If we dropped crumbs on the grass the birds would eat them, if any birds came in through the window.

I scrounged and saved for another week and finally had seven dimes, four nickels and ten pennies, which I scotch-taped to a piece of paper. I put it into an envelope with the coupon telling them to "rush me my very own mini backyard." I used my extra money for a stamp and I did not question "mini" because I figured backyards must be much bigger than 12"x 8" and that must be the size of a small yard.

I rushed home from school the next day and there was nothing. I rushed home the next day, and the next, and by the end of the week I was tired of rushing and figured it was all a fraud and I had been cheated. The day after that, a small brown envelope was waiting for me in the mailbox.

You can't put a backyard in that, I thought. I opened it and there was a folded piece of heavy aluminum foil, a plastic bag with a label reading Magic Growing Mixture and a small envelope that said Grass Seeds.

I opened the foil. With the edges folded up to hold in the magic growing mixture, the garden was twelve inches by eight inches. How was I to know that two marks like " meant inches and one mark ' meant feet? I had not learned this in school. I got cheated. I was a victim of crooked advertising. There was no way we were going to drop our crumbs into this.

With an overflow of anger, I put the garden together and spread out the magic growing mixture and sprinkled the seeds on top, as the instructions said, and then watered it. But I had no window that got four hours of sun a day, as the instructions also said I must. So I put it on the radiator next to a window that got a little bit of light, and to my stunned, absolute disbelief, less than a week later little green things began to appear. This was near the end of winter, when the radiator was still warm, but not hot.

My gosh, I was going to have a real mini backyard. I could play marbles on it. I could grow flowers, I could get out scissors and mow the grass. It was almost like having a big backyard.

The next day was a cold day and someone turned up the heat, and when I looked at my backyard the little green things were all lying dead on a steaming bed of Magic Growing Mixture. I left it and went out to play. When you get disappointed, the best thing to do is hang out with guys who don't really care about your problems because they are trying to figure out a way to get a ball down from a roof or how to get a pop bottle open when no one has a bottle opener. Those are real problems.

A few hours later I was back home and my mother was angry at me. She had tried to open the window and knocked over the tray of dirt that I had left on the radiator. She handed me a broom and told me to clean it up. I swept and cleaned and said to myself that country living was too hard and that I should just forget it. Then I looked at the broom and had one of those realizations that come in a flash of brilliance. Einstein must have felt the same sense of amazement when he discovered that light bends. I kept looking at the broom. It was made of straw.

I got a knife and cut off some of the stalks and wiped them on my pants to clean them off. I quickly finished sweeping up the Magic Growing Mixture, then ran back outside. Three of the guys were still hanging around trying to solve the problem of what to do with the next ten minutes when I showed up.

"Just like in the book," I said. "This is the way they do it in the country." I stuck one of the straws between my teeth and made it bob up and down.

Hands shot out and the straws were spread around. We all sat down on the curb and put our straws in our mouths, then took them out, then put them back. We admired each other and said this is the way they do it in the country.

"Where'd you get these?" Tommy asked.

"From my backyard," I said, and no one asked anything else.

Garden Trimmings

You know about the multi-billion-dollar industry of diet and exercise. It is built on failure because only when customers are continually in need can the industry grow without bounds. But there actually is a way to get fit and stay healthy that will cost you nothing and will be fun, and it works. There are no books to buy, no schedules, no pills, no special foods, no right and wrong way. And I am selling you nothing.

In five minutes you will be feeling good. In fifteen minutes you will forget your problems. In twenty minutes you will be getting better. You will want to go back to it the second day and even after a week you will not be bored. In a month you will say that you never felt so good. In two months your friends will ask what your secret is.

What is it? Gardening. One of the single best ways in the world to make a new person out of yourself is to bend down close to the earth and pull out a weed, and then plant a seed and then prune a bush. Walking is wonderful. Swimming is said to be the perfect exercise. Tennis is winning if you can get time on the court. Any exercise is good and gardening may be no better than any of them.

But it was the best activity for a woman named Alice. She was very large. Actually she was obese, and with that she was sad. In truth, she was so large that she was embarrassed to leave her home. So she watched television, and while she did that she ate snacks. She had tried twenty diets, and scattered around her house were a rowing machine, a walking machine and various boxes, tubes and springs for stepping up, sitting up and bouncing up. Over time they had become hangers for her exercise clothes, which she could no longer fit into.

Behind her house was a very small plot of dirt surrounded by a fence. She had ignored it for years. It was just there, a place to store her garbage can. She had barely looked at the yard, much less walked in it. One day, just out of pure dumb luck, an advertisement for a gardening magazine was delivered to her home. It had a small packet of seeds inside. For no reason except that she was bored and the seed package had a picture of pretty flowers on it, she went into her backyard and scraped out a little patch of ground with a hoe. She didn't even bend over. She sprinkled the seeds on the ground, covered them half-heartedly with the hoe and then watered the spot.

She was lucky. It was an early, warm spring with enough rain to keep the ground wet. Alice told me later that she would not have bothered to water it a second time. Then, a week or so later, she saw little green shoots coming up. This too was a matter of luck. She happened to see the shoots on the way to putting out her garbage. At that moment she realized that something she had touched actually worked, and those tiny struggling green fingers from the earth made her feel better than she had in years.

She got out the hoe and cleared away some weeds near her seedlings. Now she had a purpose. She wanted to grow more, so she scraped away another patch of ground. She even tried to bend over to pull up some weeds. She couldn't reach the ground, so she got down on her hands and knees, which she thought was a joke. Then she had trouble getting up, and she laughed. It was sort of funny that she would go to this trouble for a seed but not for herself. But she had made room for more plants. Alice got dressed and went to a garden shop. Just being out made her feel good. She wasn't embarrassed, because she had a mission. She returned with several plants and more seeds and dug holes for the plants and spread the seeds. When she realized she had not thought about eating at all, she wanted more plants. They cost less than snack food.

It got so she could not wait to get out of bed in the morning so that she could go outside and work. She bent, she stood, she contemplated and she swung the hoe with her arms. No dumbbells to buy. No plans to join.

She barely noticed the change in herself. No, she didn't become a slender beauty. A real miracle happened: when she weighed herself a week later, she had lost three pounds.

To Alice it was like a ton. It was the first time she had lost any weight in years. In her heart she was slender. She spent a month, then two months simply working in her garden, lifting watering cans, raking and planting, and by midsummer she was able to bend over and pull up weeds and get back up on her own feet without a big groan. There was a spring in her step. Her arms had lost some of their flabbiness, and she just plain felt good.

Alice's garden is now in its fourth year and it is lush, with bushes and a tiny pond. She invites her friends to come over and have tea at a table on the grass. She has lost more than forty pounds, without joining a gym and without dieting, although she eats the vegetables that she grows, which leaves less room for candy.

She isn't going to appear on the cover of a health or glamour magazine, but she is getting stronger and says she feels better and her weight is still going down. And when her friends want to know her secret, she says all she did was plant a seed and pick a weed.

Tribute to a Weed

Despite all of the money, time, effort and frustration I have spent trying to get rid of them, I would like to praise the most wonderful plant of all. It is almost invincible. It is a medal of honour winner. It is a plant with soul. There are countless varieties of it, but they all go under the same tough name: weed. It is the perfect plant, the one that has enough courage to grow where you and I and everyone else does not want it.

It is a plant so special that you cannot buy it. Its seeds do not come in little envelopes. It is a plant that lives by laughing at us and at the rest of the plant world. It will not allow itself to be put in little pots and made a fuss over by garden clubs. It will not be cut and wrapped and decorated in florist stores and have a price tag hung around its neck.

But even in the world of weeds there are heroes, and those are the weeds that grow not in our gardens, but in the cracks of the sidewalks. They are stepped on. Their leaves are crushed. Litter is thrown over them. Even in a rainstorm their roots struggle for something to drink. When the sun is out, the concrete becomes an oven. And yet they insist on growing, squeezing their fingers into ever tinier cracks in their unforgiving prison of curbs and streets.

What makes city weeds so beautiful is that they defy what should be. They stand out, and they stand on their own. And since we will take our lessons in life wherever we can get them, let us take them from the weed.

They have nothing in their favour: no soil, no room to grow, no mulching, no fertilizer, no cultivating, no one caring. In the winter they get covered with salt, which normally would kill a plant. And then in the spring they come back, fingernail-sized life in a city almost without soil. Sometimes, if you brush away the gum wrappers and look closely enough, you can see their tiny flowers blooming along the curb.

Each sliver-sized weed patch is a garden of promise. It says that no matter how much we try to bend things our way—that is to say, no matter how much dead concrete we pour on the ground—some living force keeps fighting back.

Life without tulips and roses would be sad. But life without a sidewalk weed would be pointless.

Sleep Tight, Little Friends

I put my plants to bed just before the first frost. It was the end of autumn and it was sleep time for them. I covered them with leaves and said, "Good night, little red things," and "Good night, little green things."

I love my plants, but I do not know their store-bought names. I figure they don't know they are a *Leucanthemum maximum* or an *Alpinum lanatum*, so I don't use those names. I call them little red things and little green things and sometimes little thorny things. Actually I don't know whether they are red or green since I am colour-blind. But red and green sounds better than little grey things, which is what most of them look like to me.

Still, it was time to say goodnight and coax them to sleep for the winter. They are very lucky. They get to curl up under a blanket of soft birch and maple leaves, even though they don't know those names either. When we tried to organize it, we made nature such a complex thing.

My little red and green things only know that it feels good to have the cold night air kept out by a thick quilt that wraps all around them. If no one is looking I hum them a lullaby when I am tucking them in. I never sing to them because I don't think they know the words and I don't want my neighbours catching me. It is a fact that people who sing to their plants don't get invited to have coffee with their neighbours, and my neighbours make good coffee.

My plants fall asleep with little fuss. They never ask for a drink of water, and before I know it they have all slipped into dream world. We can only guess what they dream of. It is probably sunshine and warm days, and soft rain that falls at night and worms that tickle their roots. And for what we call those best of all exciting dreams, they dream of bees and butterflies that crawl deep in their flowers and then wiggle. Of course there must be nightmares too, pruning scissors and weed whackers and chemicals dumped on their heads, but it is a long sleep and they have time to get back to bees and butterflies.

While they sleep, they miss the Christmas rush. They miss the shovelling of snow. They miss traffic jams when the heater, defroster, windshield wipers, radio and horn are all going at once. All they know is that their blanket feels so good that they don't even have to roll over.

There is another reason that I put my plants to sleep. When the winter gets too cold and the tax forms arrive and the Christmas bills come in and the car insurance rates go up, I think of my little red and green friends snuggled in so comfortably, and I say move over, let me escape with you.

I close my eyes and pull a thick blanket up to my nose and dream of butterflies and bees, and suddenly tax forms and bills don't seem so bad, at least not for a little while. So when I put my plants to bed it was restful, and not just for those getting tucked in.

The Beetle Battle

One summer I had a little problem with my garden. It wasn't with the plants, but with my neighbour, who thought I was wacko.

It started when I was looking at some of my bushes and noticed that the leaves had holes in them. I went to my neighbourhood garden centre and the salesperson said the problem was caused by a little beetle, a leaf-eating beetle. I should buy this powder, she told me, and spread it on the ground, and buy this sticky tape and wrap it around the bottoms of the bushes, and after that I would have no trouble.

So I bought the powder and the tape and I powdered and taped, and then I watched more of the leaves on my bushes turning into fine lace. It takes several applications, I was told. Those are tough little critters.

They were having dinner on my rhododendrons, hiking with their knives and plates up the thick old stems to their banquet tables. They had a midnight snack on the hedges that line a walkway in my yard. Then they ordered takeout on my Joe Pye weed, which was a gift from a friend. It grows so fast it is like a Jack and the beanstalk plant. It was gaining two inches a day on the top but losing an inch of leaves a day on the bottom.

I researched beetles in that well of all natural information, the *National Geographic*. I looked through the two hundred issues I had been saving just in case I ever needed to know something, and after less than an hour, during which I read about spiders and quilting bees, I found *BEETLES*. I learned that they were here before the dinosaurs and that they are among the greatest survival success stories in the history of this planet.

Oh, wonderful. Me alone, up against a champion survivor with 200 million years of victories behind it. I learned there are beetles that live underwater by breathing from bubbles of air they capture and hold under their wings. And there are beetles that survive in the desert by drinking the morning dew that condenses on their backs. Great, I thought, beetles are smarter and tougher and more adaptable than me.

And there are beetles that live by eating and digesting wood, and others that eat dead animals, and some that live off nothing but dung, the one food they don't have to fight over. And then there was a picture of a beetle that eats leaves. My enemy! And now I had his wanted poster.

The article explained how beetle collectors get their beetles. They spread a blanket under a bush and shake the branches and the beetles fall out and they scoop them up. Now give me a little time not to be embarrassed for not thinking of this myself. But my wife Valerie said no way was I going to use one of our blankets to snuggle up with strange beetles, some of which may be female. So I got a cardboard box instead. No tape, no powder, but still leading to the end of the road for beetles. I had to wait until night fell because leaf-eating beetles get hungry only after the sun goes down. I went to war armed with my box and a flashlight.

But now picture this from the neighbour's window. He looks out into the darkness over his evening tea and suddenly he sees the beam of a flashlight moving up and down inside a bush. He should have known it was someone looking for leaf-eating beetles, and if he read *National Geographic* he would have known.

"Hello?" It was my neighbour, speaking to me over the fence. Apparently he doesn't read *National Geographic*. "Is anyone there?"

"I'm hunting for beetles," I said. "Leaf-eating beetles."

"OK," he said. "I thought maybe you were a burglar or something."

"Nope, just hunting for beetles," I said.

The next night I was back at it again. Anything that has outlived the dinosaurs will take more than one safari to drive into backyard extinction. Shake, plunk, squish. The hunt, the capture and the execution all in one location.

My neighbour looked out his window again.

"Beetles?" he said.

"Yup, beetles," I said.

And the third night. "Beetles again?"

"Yup."

And the fourth night, and the fifth. I didn't care how silly I looked, because after a week I was winning. Fewer and fewer beetles were falling into the box, and some hole-free leaves were beginning to grow on the bushes.

The next morning there was a knock on my door. Jimmy, the six-year-old son of my neighbour, was standing there. "My daddy says you've been hunting for beetles," he said. Then he handed me a jar he had been holding behind his back. It was full of beetles, all kinds of beetles, including leaf-eating beetles. "I collected them for you," he said.

"Jimmy," I said to him. "I want to thank you for helping to restore the balance of nature. With people like you around, beetles haven't a care in the world."

WEEd TREE

When my uncle died, I went back to New York for his funeral. Uncle Ed was a good man. He was a Mason, he was a deacon of his church, he was a bus driver and he was a scrappy guy. Before buses he drove coal delivery trucks that had chain-link transmissions, which looked like giant bicycle sprockets and a chain the size of your arm, turning the back wheels. Driving buses was cleaner work, and he liked joking with people. Later he taught bus drivers how to drive buses.

When I heard about his death, I booked a flight for the next day. I would arrive at the funeral home on the last night of the wake, back in the neighbourhood where I grew up. I had left there a long time ago for life here, and that was a good choice. There is concrete. Here is grass and mountains and trees.

The morning before I left for the funeral I walked around my garden in Vancouver and spotted one of those weed trees growing in my vegetable patch. The real name of the tree is sumac, but most call them weeds, big weeds, because like all weeds they come uninvited and grow where you don't want them. They grow fast and have leaves that

look like outstretched fingers. I said that I would cut it
down as soon as I got back

I landed at Kennedy airport at 7:30 p.m., in plenty of
time to get to the funeral home. But something was different. There was confusion in the air and more lineups than
usual. People were shouting and pushing and the crowds
were growing.

"What's going on?"

"The taxis have just gone on strike," someone said.

"What? How can I get to Queens?" I said in panic.

Well, actually I couldn't, at least not inside ninety minutes. I would have to take a bus or a subway to Manhattan
and then take a train back. That would be about two hours
of riding.

Bad does not begin to describe the situation. Awful does
not come close. My aunt and my cousin were at the funeral
home, expecting me. But worst of all, I would not get to see
my uncle's face one last time. I got on a bus.

"You sure look sad," said the driver.

I told him why.

"I know that funeral home," he said.

"Yes?" I said, a little surprised. New York is very big
and has many funeral homes.

"So your uncle was a bus driver?" he said.

"Yup," I said, possibly with self-pity.

The bus filled up and he pulled away. We got on Van
Wyck Expressway, which leads to Manhattan. I had taken
this route before. In an hour I would be at Grand Central
Station. Another hour after that I would be walking up to a
darkened funeral home.

At Jamaica Avenue the bus turned. I looked up—something was wrong. I knew that route very well and I knew that the driver was not supposed to get off the expressway at Jamaica Avenue. The other passengers knew it too. They looked out the windows and at each other in surprise, and I heard someone ask the driver whether this was the bus to Manhattan.

I could just barely hear him saying, in his Spanish accent, ". . . small detour."

We drove under the elevated train along a street I had grown up on. I was back home. I could not really be here; this could not be so. But it was. Ten blocks later the bus pulled over and the driver said, shouting above the heads of the crowd, "The fellow going to the funeral. You can get a bus at this corner that will take you there."

I squeezed my way through the other passengers and thanked him with words that did not come out right. "Thank you, thank you." That is not enough. Maybe my eyes said more. I got off and he pulled away and turned at the next corner and was gone, back toward Van Wyck Expressway and Manhattan. He would be ten minutes behind schedule. He might probably make it up by speeding or he might dismiss it with a shrug. I will never know.

I got to the funeral home half an hour before the doors closed, and said goodbye.

I stayed with my Aunt Chris for a week after the burial, and we talked about her husband almost constantly. She told me many stories about this man, who was a meat-and-potatoes-and-no-vegetables guy who loved football and baseball. The drawers in his dresser held more tools than socks.

They had been married for almost sixty years. He helped with the dishes and put out the garbage and did housework. And when his wife got frail he did the laundry—his laundry, anyway, but not her frilly things. There he drew the line in the sand of wash day. He would hang out his underwear, but not hers. Some things were a little too psychologically heavy for even his big hands to lift.

But she told me about the day a month or so before he died, when she was at the window hanging out her things. She was using her clothespins, which she kept in the large brown tin cans that had once held powdered baby food. She had mixed it up for her son when he was an infant. He was at retirement age now. Aunt Chris did not like change. She had just finished putting the last clothespin on the last piece of frilly underwear when the pulley holding the line came out of the wall. It had put in many decades of service and this was the day and the hour and the minute when it quit.

My aunt grabbed the end of the line—luckily only her things were on it, so it was light—and she shouted for Ed.

"Let it go," he said from behind her. "You don't have to hold it."

"No," she said. "I just washed them and I am not going to let them get dirty."

"Don't be silly, you can't stand there holding the line."

Picture it: she is leaning out the window holding the clothesline. He cannot get past her to grab the line, and she will not let go.

So the big football fan and man who drove trucks filled with coal and buses filled with people, did the only thing he could. He went outside, walked through the alley and

183

around back, and in full view of the neighbours, while his wife lowered the line, he unpegged each piece of her underwear, took it off the line and laid it over his shoulder. Then he walked past his audience once again and went back into the house.

Putting up a new line was easy. That's the kind of work he liked. But carrying that frilly underwear on a shoulder that had once lifted barrels of coal was one of those heroic moments that seem so ridiculous at the time. But then you never forget it.

I listened to that story while my aunt and I walked around her block. They lived in what is called a rapidly changing neighbourhood, meaning graffiti and litter and broken-down cars and less than pleasant people were not in short supply. The stores that were still in business had steel shutters over their windows, even during the day. But many shop owners had given up, put padlocks on their front doors and walked away.

The elevated train ran overhead with much noise and little sunlight getting through. It was not a great place for those who like to see the miracles of nature. But right at the corner of my aunt and uncle's block, right under the elevated train, right next to an abandoned machine shop, was a grate in the sidewalk. It was an open shaft for letting light and air into the apartments below ground. It had steel bars across the top to keep people from falling in. Because no one had cleaned out the hole for years, it was half-filled with litter—newspapers, candy and cigarette wrappings, broken glass. But it had one other thing that made me stop and look. It had one of those miracles that nature is so good at.

Growing from that mass of rotting, festering garbage was a tree, a weed tree—a sumac, apparently, with its roots sunk deep into the muck and its branches reaching up toward the steel bars.

It must have been there for a few years because its trunk looked solid and about as thick as a child's arm. The trunk was always in the shade, but some sunshine got just far enough under the bars to touch the leaves that were reaching up to it. It is not stretching a point to say that the sumac was sort of like my uncle and that bus driver, simply doing what they had to do when they had to do it.

A week later I returned to Vancouver and went into my backyard and looked at the sumac tree. But I did not pick up my saw. Instead, I strung some Christmas lights on it. Anything from a family that tough and determined has the right to live wherever it chooses. I can move my vegetable garden. I will get more nourishment, at least for my spirit, out of that tree.

Under Canvas in Paradise

Usually the best things about travelling are the ones that go wrong. They are annoying. They are a pain. And they are what you talk about later. This one started when I figured out that the only way we could go to Hawaii was to camp.

"Cool," said our kids.

"Camping?" queried my wife Valerie. "What if it rains?"

"No way," I said. "Look at this." I showed her a magazine ad with a smiling family standing by their tent on the beach. "It's always sunny in Hawaii."

We signed up and paid ahead of time, and in Maui we picked up a tent, cots, a camping stove and a Volkswagen Beetle to get to the campground. The kids had to sit on top of our sleeping bags and knapsacks.

"Comfy?" I asked.

"We can't see anything," came two voices.

Then we stopped for groceries. "Can we get this chocolate cake?" asked Sean, who was nine. The cake had chocolate filling and chocolate icing over its chocolate body. "Please," he begged. It was a vacation, so we said all right. "All *right*!" he fired back. It is good to make someone happy on a vacation.

"Can we have a piece soon?"

"Nooo. Not until after dinner."

"Awww."

It is bad to have complaining on a vacation. But we thought we would be at the campground in a little more than an hour. It was only eighty kilometres away. What we didn't know was that we had to take a road that had the curves of a ribbon that someone had dropped on the ground. The road to Hana has more than one hundred downshifting, brake-grinding, steering wheel-yanking turns. Plus it's narrow.

And then it started to rain.

"I don't feel good," said our daughter Colleen, who was eleven.

"Me too," said Sean, who was holding the cake box in his sweaty hands.

After three hours of swaying back and forth and forward and back and back and forth and pulling over so that what was in the stomach could come out, followed by more swaying back and forth, we drove into the campground. We were so happy to get there that we missed the little sign that said: No Drinking Water Available. We did notice that we were on a cliff about a quarter mile above the ocean.

"Can we have some cake now?"

"No," we said, trying to be patient. We told the kids to find the way to the beach while we put up the tent. When we unpacked it, we discovered that it was still wet from the last folks who had rented it. "If I promise not to complain, would you promise not to complain?" Valerie said.

Then the kids came back with the news: there was no

way to get to the beach. This was just a viewpoint camp-ground. And there was no water. We had carried no water with us. Bottled water had not yet become a way of life, and all we had brought was a couple of cans of ginger ale. Campgrounds are supposed to have water, aren't they? We sent the kids out with a pot and a prayer. We could see other campers. Say please, we told them while we continued try-ing to pull the wet canvas over the aluminum poles.

"At least it stopped raining," I said.

"But if it was raining, we could get water in the pots," said Valerie.

"Is that complaining?" I asked.

"No, it's observing."

"My hands are cold," I said.

"That's complaining," she said.

But before she could take advantage of my complaint with a comment about my choice of vacations, the kids came back. They had less than half a pot of water. "This is all they said they could spare," said Colleen. For dinner that night we had canned soup, canned beans, canned ginger ale and bread.

Before we finished eating, the rain came back. It came in solid walls of water. It came with thunder and streaks of lightning, and as we sat inside the tent, the roof started to leak. Sean was sitting on a cot, holding a flashlight and look-ing at the cake, which had been banged around so much most of the icing was gone. "We'll cut it as soon as we get a plastic cover over us," we said.

In the driving rain, my wife and I pulled the groundsheet from under the tent and spread it over the top and tied it down. We got back inside and watched the roof being forced down by troughs of water caught in the new cover. Then outside again to empty the troughs and pull the tarp tighter and then tie it again. My jacket was soaked and water was running down under my shirt and into the crotch of my pants.

"I will not complain," I said to myself.

"I hate this," Valerie shouted.

"Bless you," I said.

"What?" She couldn't hear me over the wind and rain.

"Bless you," I said.

"For what?"

"For complaining. My crotch is soaked."

"What do I care?" she said.

Then we crawled back into the tent to see Colleen sitting on the plastic picnic cooler because water was filling the bottom of the tent.

"Can we have some cake now?" Sean asked.

What a brilliant idea! In Hawaii, in a tent lit only by flashlights, with our feet in water, our sleeping bags soaked and rain coming through the sides, we ate the cake and drank the last ginger ale.

More than twenty years later, whenever we talk about that vacation, not one of us mentions the beaches we eventually got to or the museums we visited. We talk about that cake and the rainstorm, and we laugh. It is a memory that even outlasted the pukka shells.

A Restful Weekend
at a Cabin in the Woods

There are many people who go for relaxing weekends at their cabins in the woods. I used to long for that myself, until some friends invited us to their cabin in the woods.

"It will be very relaxing," they said. "There is nothing to do."

They are Barb and Vern, a nice couple who worked hard to get their cabin in the woods. It has no electricity, so no TV and no radio. "Bring lots to read," they said.

They invited two couples. Ruth and Gunther brought some books and Scrabble and a chessboard, since Gunther loves chess, and Vern said there would be nothing to break his concentration. Valerie and I went with our sleeping bags and two books each and several magazines. We bought a couple more magazines before we boarded the ferry so that we wouldn't use up the first ones before we got there.

Barb and Vern's cabin is at Skookumchuck, at the end of Sechelt Narrows, one of the most beautiful places on earth, with trees that kiss the edge of water, which wraps itself around the land like a lover. To get there we took the ferry from Horseshoe Bay, and that was an exciting trip because Vern talked and talked about their cabin and the peace and quiet to be found there. "It is a great place to lose the big-city jitters," he said. "You come back feeling like a new person." He was so excited telling us about the cabin that we arrived at the dock at Langdale without having had a moment to go out on deck and gaze at the islands passing by.

The drive up the Sunshine Coast to Sechelt, where they kept their boat, was a little hectic because, according to Vern, we had to get to the cabin early enough to have a leisurely lunch. Otherwise we would be eating too close to dinner and then we would feel rushed. At Sechelt we had to go shopping, and Vern said that if we split up we could get it done quicker. Valerie and I would get the propane, Vern and Barb the groceries and Ruth and Gunther the wine. "I don't want to rush you, but try to hurry," he said. "We don't want to waste a minute that we could spend at the cabin."

And then, because of the hurry we were in, we had an hour-long boat ride with the motor at full throttle. Full throttle in a seventeen-foot outboard means you can only shout, "Look at that."

"What? I can't hear you."

"Never mind."

"What?"

At the other end we had to move the supplies out of the boat. There were blankets and tools and pillows and food, and they moved to the shore and up to the cabin by wheelbarrow and shoulder and bucket brigade. Now, please don't think I am complaining. It was wonderful exercise, and when we finally made the last trip and carried the books and games to the peace of the cabin, I was ready to relax.

"Since there is nothing to do," said our host, "we thought we would take you on a little hike." Barb had made some sandwiches so that we could enjoy the scenery and eat at the same time. "There is so much we want you to see," said Barb. "We can rest in the cabin later."

I looked back at the pretty cabin, which truly was pretty, as we walked farther and farther away from it up an old logging road. We saw big trees and climbed over fallen trees and got wet crossing creeks, and several hours later we returned and I was ready to relax.

But Vern said that this was the only chance he would have to fix the emergency oar for the boat, which had broken on the last trip. Gunther and I volunteered to help. We found a piece of metal pipe and shaved down the ends of the broken oar. We squeezed and pushed and banged, and in time the broken oar became a fixed oar with a metal bandage. And now I was ready to relax.

But it was time to cook dinner, and we had a communal cook over the propane stove. Cooking with friends is always fun. There was a lot of laughter and we looked like bees cutting and mixing and boiling and frying. Bees get the work done, but they don't know much about relaxing.

After dinner there was cleaning up to do, and with friends that is also fun. It became like a party, with washing and drying and stacking and joking, and lighting lanterns because it was getting dark.

"Let's go down to the beach," said Vern. "It's like a scary movie without going to the theatre."

We stepped out into the woods, which now were pitch dark. Our gas lanterns made long shadows and Vern said there were bears in the woods and if we heard one, we should stand still. Then there was a crashing sound nearby.

"Aaahhh!" That was the sound of several women and men shrieking. It was followed by the sound of Vern laughing. He had thrown a stick into the woods.

"Enough, I'm exhausted," I said. "I'm going to bed."

Back in the cabin, Vern said he would give us each some privacy. He got out some blankets and a hammer and nails, then pounded away in the corners of the cabin to hang the blankets and create makeshift rooms. He was very kind. He was very noisy. I crawled into my sleeping bag and fell into a deep sleep, which ended bright and early with the sound of an axe thumping through wood.

I went to the door of the cabin. Vern was outside, whacking away at a pile of logs. "What are you doing?"

"Making a fire for you to wake up to."

"Couldn't you make it later?"

"It would be too late then," he said. "We're going for a boat ride."

I have to admit that the ride through the rapids was exciting. At one point I was trying to take a picture, and my camera went up and I went down and I tried to hold onto the back of a seat where there is nothing to hold onto as the boat went up again and then down again, then up, then down. It was like a roller coaster without the safety bar. It would be good to relax after this.

But after the boat ride we only had time to eat lunch and then to get ready to leave. But first we had to burn all the garbage, sweep the cabin, pack the groceries and carry them by wheelbarrow and shoulder and bucket brigade back to the boat. Then we had an hour-long ride at full throttle so that we could get to Sechelt in time to drive to Langdale to catch the ferry.

At Sechelt the tide was too low to get the boat back onto the boat trailer. We tried to lengthen the launch pad by putting rocks into the water so that the trailer could back out farther, and it worked. We got the boat up on the trailer, but it was crooked. Gunther and Vern and I stood in the water up to our chests trying to straighten the boat by rocking it while Barb sat behind the wheel of their truck, looking at her watch.

"I hope we don't miss the next ferry. It's the last one," she said.

We got the boat straightened, then raced down the road with hundreds of other cars, all trying to make the same unforgiving deadline. All I can say is that we were lucky they put on an extra sailing. Many hours later, we got home and unpacked our books.

The next day at work I was asked why I looked so exhausted.

Exhausted? I just had a relaxing weekend at a cabin in the woods. I only hope I don't get invited again soon. They are nice people and their cabin is pretty. But one more relaxing weekend and I'll need a week off to recover.

A Short Drive into the Past

Sometimes you don't have to travel very far to see how the world can turn upside down. And the upside down can be very nice. Valerie and I had been invited for lunch in Maple Ridge. It was about a half hour drive away, and it was a trip into the Twilight Zone.

But we didn't know it. We sat around the table complaining about Canadian politicians and the falling dollar and the high price of gasoline. Then we got onto the subject of air travel, and one of the women, Alison, said that her father had been a pilot. In fact, he was a Spitfire pilot in the Battle of Britain, "shooting down Germans," she said.

That was an uncomfortable moment. The host, Gunther, the man who had relaxed at the cabin with us, is German. He was born in Germany during the war. His father had been in the German army, a foot soldier and one of the tens of miserable thousands of anonymous men in the battle of Stalingrad. They were trying to force the Russians inside the city to starve to death, while they were freezing to death outside.

Across the table from Gunther was Boris, who was also born during the war, in Russia, and who, like most Russians, was brought up to hate Germans. Gunther and Boris play chess together. Next to Boris sat Howard, born in Canada but raised during his childhood in an internment camp in the interior of BC because he is of Japanese descent. During the war some of his relatives were still in Japan. One of them was believed to be in the navy, which means he would have been on a ship in the Pacific hunting for American ships.

I sat across the table from Howard. In 1944 and '45 my father was on an island somewhere in the Pacific, waiting to shoot Japanese soldiers.

"Good God," someone joked. "Our relatives and parents were all trying to kill each other."

"Glad they missed," someone else said.

Suddenly the falling dollar and the stupid politicians did not matter so much. All countries have problems. But a lunch like this, at a table surrounded by friends, could happen nowhere else on earth except Canada.

Library Tax

Mrs. Brazil started walking to town. She had eighteen miles to go. She held her hand out when a pickup truck came by and got a ride for more than twelve miles, which was a salvation. But she had to walk the rest of the way, which took her almost two hours, and when she got to the courthouse it was too late. Court was finished for the day. Without eating and without buying a cup of coffee she turned around and she walked back home, carrying her summons to appear in court. Court was in Haney and she lived in a shack in Whonnock. She was summoned to court because she had not paid her library tax of seventy-five cents.

It was 1944. Her husband was with the First Division of the Canadian army, fighting for his country. While she was walking he lay in an army hospital in England, recovering from his wounds. He would soon go back into battle. He had been gone so long that he had never seen his own twin girls, his daughters. They had been born after he was shipped out. They were four years old now.

His wife—and there is no name, only the initials R.W.— Mrs. R. W. Brazil, fed the children from what she grew in her garden and not much else. She may have been Ruth, she may have been Ruby, she certainly was tough: two kids, no husband, no money, and typical of many women during the war. The only reason there is any memory of her at all is because of a brief article torn from a newspaper in anger by a man who did not know her, kept for fifty-eight years, then shown to his niece, who showed it to me. Sometimes history survives by threads.

Over the decades, even the reason why Frank Aicken tore out that story changed. Frank was a lumberman. He has lived in Whonnock since the 1920s, watching it grow from a remote village to being incorporated with more than a half dozen surrounding towns into Maple Ridge, with malls and concrete and traffic jams. And while his town changed, his country changed. We now sentence criminals to very light fines and jail terms, making punishment a distant second to reform. You can kill someone, stab them twenty times, get a life sentence and spend seven years in jail. You can be arrested with a pocket full of cocaine and never go behind bars.

Frank is upset by this leniency and showed his niece, Ruth, the yellowing news story, printed before she was born. "This was how justice used to be done," he said. The story said that Mrs. Brazil was being sent to Oakalla prison because she had not paid her library tax. It said that she had missed her court appearance, and because of that she was fined six dollars. That was more than a day's pay, and she said she could not afford it.

The judge, William F. Armstrong of Websters Corners, was quoted in the newspaper as saying, "We are not asking much, but the law must be carried out. If we refuse to prosecute her it will mean that every other resident in the district can also refuse to pay [the tax]." He said he had no alternative but to send her to jail. "We must enforce the law." That was the iron hand of justice.

Frank wanted this to be a lesson on how staunch the law once was. But it turned out to be a lesson of a different kind. He told his niece that when he had originally read the story he was so angry at the law for sending Mrs. Brazil to jail that he wanted to do something. But what? There were no protests in the street then. He did not know the woman. And the law was the law. But when the tax collector came to his door, he said, "Go away. If that poor woman, Mrs. Brazil, is going to jail for not paying, I'm not paying."

Then he told his friends what he had done, and he had many friends. And he must have done a good job of telling them, because in a short time almost no one in Whonnock was paying their library tax. Public action is an incredibly powerful tool. It can bend rules and laws and courts, and sometimes knock them out cold and change everything. The tax was rescinded and Mrs. Brazil, who was appealing her sentence, did not go to jail.

The great thing about that old article is not that it reminds us of how hard justice once was. The great thing is that one man, who never took credit for it, saved a woman from an unjust fate, and helped make a government, even if it was only a local government, change its policy.

We talk about needing big changes in our systems, about reforming our governments and courts from the top down. I don't think so. What we need is more people like Frank.

Travels With Mack

I always thought I had been on a lot of good car trips. I've driven the Alaska Highway a couple of times, and made more than a dozen crossings of Canada and the US. But then my friend John told me about the trips he and his friends took more than thirty years ago in a beat-up International Harvester pickup truck, and he left me far in his dust.

This pack of young travellers found the truck in a worn-out garage in a back lane in their neighbourhood. In the world of practical transportation, it was perfect for them. If only they could get their hands on it, this hunk of black and grey and red tin would fulfill all their travel dreams. There was no place it could not take them.

The door to the garage was wide open and covered with vines. It would never close again. At first the kids were afraid to go in, but one boy did, then another, and the lure of the truck pulled them all in. It needed some work. It had a lot of rust. Its tires were flat, and when the kids looked through the grille, they could see only space—it had no motor. But when you are eight and nine years old, you can't use a motor anyway.

"That's my truck."

They jumped. A lady as old as their grandmothers stood there watching them.

"My husband and I drove that everywhere. But that was a long time ago," she said.

"It's a nice truck," said one of the girls.

"It was my favourite."

"Can we play in it?" asked a boy.

The old lady nodded, and the first automotive deal in the lives of these kids was done. No cash, no forms, no inspection and no insurance. "But drive safely," she said.

The words were a magic spell. "Did you hear that?" one boy said. "She told us to drive safely. That's what big people say."

They walked around the truck, touching it and running their hands over the curves of the fenders. They were in love with their first vehicle. If a new car company had filmed the scene they could use it to sell anything on wheels.

"We got to have a name for it," someone said.

"Daisy."

"No, that's a girl's name, and girls don't look like this."

Their faces screwed up. They wouldn't go for a drive until they had a name.

"How about Mack?" someone said.

Perfect. A tough, rusty name for a tough old hunk of rust. They all agreed, because when you get the name right it sounds like it always belonged.

They opened the door and it squeaked and groaned, and it made the same squeak and groan at the start and end of every trip the kids took. In the cab the seat was ripped and the stuffing was coming out. It had no radio, just a hole in the dashboard.

But what it did have was a steering wheel, a clutch and a gearshift. The brake pedal was no good. It was flat on the floor, and the gas pedal had broken off. But those devices were too much to worry about anyway, when you had to remember to push down on the clutch, which you did by sliding off the seat so your foot could reach it, and then change the gear and still keep the steering wheel moving back and forth. Driving was not easy back in the old days. None of the kids was sure what gear to put it in, but they all knew they had to keep changing gears or they would never get to where they were going.

Although Mack never got any air in his tires, a half dozen kids toured bumpy back roads in him, and drove through big cities and over mountains. They drove all summer, and when the leaves started falling they took more trips. They kept going deep into the winter until it got too cold to go any farther. The only heater they had was their mittens. They had near misses and ran out of gas, and they picked up hitchhikers and got lost. And just as they had learned in their family cars, the boys said they could find their way without stopping to ask for directions.

By the time John got through telling me about his road trips in that old pickup, I knew there were a lot of places I still had to get to, but I would never find the way. The problem is the universal problem: my car has a motor and spark plugs, and if they don't work I worry. That is just too much weight for a magic carpet, especially one already crowded with the dreams of kids.

Hurry Up, We're Late

I was in Victoria and was hoping to catch the five o'clock ferry home. I had a lot of work to get done back in Vancouver, and I knew if I hoped for the five I might make the seven. I admire people who get to places on time, because they are not like me: they do not sweat and worry and raise their blood pressure. Somehow they have figured out how to start early enough to get to where they are going on time. It seems easy, and it is a good way to live.

People who are on time know what movies are about because they get there at the beginning. It is after the double agent has shot the spy and taken over his identity that I am stumbling my way through the dark theatre looking for a seat. And when others are saying, "Ohhh, now it all makes sense" when the double agent reveals the truth, I am saying "Huh?" People who are late don't win prizes for being bright. And when someone invites me to dinner I generally ruin the first course by missing it, and then I try to eat fast to catch up, which hurts my stomach. In short, people like me who are late are unforgivable social bums.

I know I must change, and I thought of this at quarter to

five while I was still drinking coffee with a friend in Victoria. Darn, I had missed the ferry. But I would be on time for the seven o'clock sailing. So I asked for a refill, the deadly second cup, and went on with the conversation with my friend.

"Whoops," he said at six. The conversation had been very good. "You better get going."

"No problem," I said. "An hour for a half-hour drive."

"Plus the lineup."

Lineup? On a Sunday night?

"Only people who get there early get on," he said.

Zoom, how fast can I drive without speeding more than everyone else who is speeding? How fast can I go without being dangerous and without raising my blood pressure? Why am I always late?

Twenty-five minutes later I pulled up to the ticket booth.

"I can't guarantee you'll get on the seven," said the nice lady who took my money.

"I will, I will, I will." Positive thought works, doesn't it? I can will the ferry to have room for me.

The line moved and stopped and moved and stopped, with ten cars in front of me. They tried to squeeze a few more on. "I will make it. I will, I will." Nine cars, eight. I was counting, because counting would make them all get on. Seven, six, five. The woman stopping the cars got a radio call. I could see her nodding. She waved ahead numbers four, and three, and two.

One car in front of me. My breathing was coming quick and I pushed that car on the ferry with my fingers moving over the steering wheel. That always works. She waved it ahead. Great! I moved, and she put her hand up. "Sorry." She dropped an orange cone in front of my bumper, shrugged in apology and walked away.

"How long?" I asked through the window. Maybe they were putting on another sailing and maybe it wouldn't be too long.

She heard me and turned. "Two hours."

Darn. I said other things too. I stood in line and got a coffee, but I didn't want another coffee. I sat and then walked in circles, and finally I promised myself that if I did nothing else in life, I would be on time from now on. Definitely, positively, I swore to myself.

Three months later nine o'clock arrived, and I was the first on the ship with my new goal firmly in place. I sat in one of the chairs on the upper deck, closed my eyes and thought of all the things I would accomplish because from now on I would be on time. The ferry sailed and I was content, except for all the work that I was now behind on.

"Wow, did you see that?" Many voices were speaking at once.

I opened my eyes and I could not believe what I saw. The entire sky, across the western horizon, was on fire. The sun blazed into the ocean with reds and oranges making moving paintings on the walls inside the ferry. I went outside along with hundreds of other passengers and watched a light show so brilliant no words could hold its spirit. It burst from the water and grabbed the darkness. Cameras were clicking all along the deck, but what they caught in one moment grew into something much greater the next. Flames of mixed reds and yellows disappeared when streaks of orange grew from nowhere. God or nature or whatever you take the creator of that sunset to be is one heck of an artist. The show almost had a plot, from birth to life to fading. It was a heavenly display that we got to witness without the inconvenience of dying.

Then I thought of all the poor people who had caught the seven o'clock ferry. I was sad for them. Everyone should have seen this. From now on, I vowed, I would always order that second cup of coffee.

Thirsting for a Living

This is a travel tip: Instead of looking for cities with big buildings or expensive theme parks, I suggest you visit a drugstore.

This is no ordinary store, though. It is in America, in the Badlands of South Dakota, an area so dry and desolate and hot in the summer that you would think you were on a back road in Saskatchewan in August. There is nothing to visit for a hundred miles before you get to this drugstore or after you leave it, but it is an entrepreneurial work of genius.

It is called Wall Drugs, and it all started during the Great Depression, when a couple inherited a one-room pharmacy in a town with only a few thousand people living in it. As the Depression went on, the town got smaller and the drugstore was lucky to sell a couple of bottles of aspirin a week.

So the new owners used the only tool they had, their imagination, to find some way to draw in all the people who just passed by on the highway without a glance. They did not have an amusement park or a golf course or a museum. But they did have one thing, the wife said: they had water coming out of the tap in their kitchen. This was long before cars had air conditioning. If they could give the water away to hot and thirsty travellers, she thought, the hot and thirsty travellers would appreciate it, and they might buy something.

They put up signs at each end of the road leading into town. Here is the genius. They would not just give away water, but it would be "Free Water." And not just Free Water, but "Free Ice Water," even if it did not have ice in it. That is what the signs said: Free Ice Water. Wall Drugs. People go to marketing courses for years and do not learn this kind of lesson: it is called using what you have.

Before they could get back to their store after putting up the signs, the couple had people pulling up to get free ice water. Some bought packages of gum, and some purchased tissues to wipe their sweat away.

Well, if business is good with two signs, the smart thing to do is increase the advertising. They drove five miles down the road and put signs up that read: Only Five Miles to Wall Drugs, Free Ice Water. Then they put up more signs farther down the road: Ten Miles to Go for Free Ice Water at Wall Drugs.

They started to get customers who reported that they had been looking forward to getting there. They had started getting thirsty reading the signs and they wanted their water, and maybe they would buy something.

That was a long time ago. Now, if you are driving on Interstate 90 through South Dakota, you will see billboards that say: Only 300 Miles to Go to Wall Drugs. Free Ice Water. And, a little while later: Wall Drugs. 250 Miles

Ahead. Free Ice Water. You will get to the point where you say, "I wonder when the next sign's coming up?" And there it will be: Don't Miss Your Free Ice Water at Wall Drugs. Only 200 Miles to Go.

Then you will pull into the town of Wall, which now has an industry: Wall Drugs. The store is three blocks long and covers both sides of the street. Almost everyone in town makes a living there. You can buy black velvet paintings of Elvis, and "authentic" Indian jewellery and Hummel figures and chewing gum and Western clothing and saddles for horses and aspirin, and you can eat a plate of bacon and eggs and write postcards sent "From Wall Drugs."

They are now building their second two-storey motel for people who drive hundreds and sometimes thousands of miles to stop at Wall Drugs. And yes, you still can get all the free ice water you want. They give it to you in plastic cups—which are also free.

I would guess that most people who get a free cup of water wind up spending $20 or $25 on t-shirts and lunch and postcards.

Someday, if you get there, you might also buy a package of mints or a hamburger. But what you will really go away with is the idea that nothing is actually impossible. If there was one good idea out there like that, there must be hundreds, or even thousands more just waiting to be thought of. The secret is, you just have to be thirsty enough to look for them.

THE FINISH LINE

One of the most-remembered trips I ever heard of was one block long and straight downhill. Mike Louie told me about it, at the same time he told me about his fear that he was getting to be just like his father. He adores his father, but just because you love your father doesn't mean you actually want to be like him, and it is a shock when you find you are becoming him.

Mike made the discovery when he moved back home for a while in his mid-thirties. It occasionally happens that when you walk back in through your old front door, you can see yourself looking like the people waiting for you.

On his first morning back home, he decided to surprise his father by cleaning out the garage. His father was famous for putting stuff in his garage and taking nothing out. Mike opened the garage door and, "Omigod, there was a mountain of things," he told me. He would conquer it, and he would help his father. So he rolled up his sleeves and went to work. The closest thing to him was a bucket of old spark plugs. His father had used the plugs for sinkers when he went fishing. But he had not gone fishing for years, and he had enough sinkers to last a lifetime. So Mike dragged out the bucket.

Behind it were plumbing pipes, and old tires and rope and plastic flowerpots. He got sweaty and dirty hauling them outside. He found an old pair of sunglasses and a rusty key ring—probably the locks had long ago been sawed off after the keys were lost. And there were more plastic pots. His father had once been an ardent gardener, but that was years ago and the garden was overgrown now. Mike kept moving stuff out until he had a mountain in the driveway.

"What do you think you are doing?" His father's voice came from an open window, and it was not pleased.

"Getting rid of this junk for you."

"That's not junk," said his father.

Mike held up a spark plug.

"When I'm ready to go fishing I'll use them," his father said. He closed the window and came outside, working his way between his son and his treasures.

Mike pointed to the sunglasses.

"I was looking for them," said his father, and he put them in his pocket.

"Why are you keeping the pipes?"

"To make irrigation for the garden."

"But you haven't done anything in the garden for years."

"When I do, I'll be ready."

Then his father asked Mike if he remembered his first bicycle, "the one you learned to ride on." They climbed through the stuff to one side of the garage, and there, between boards and an old door, was a small red bike. "And remember the dollhouse we made for your sister?"

211

His father pointed to the roof of the dollhouse, sticking up from a neighbourhood of paint cans. "When I'm gone you can get rid of this stuff. Until then, it is my diary."

Then Mike caught sight of two wheels and a box that had once been part of a soapbox car. "I remember that!" he said.

His father had helped him build it. But his father was also then running a corner grocery store, a job that started before the milkmen got up and ended after the movie ushers at the late show went home. There was not much time left over for building go-karts, but Mike had wanted to be in the race, so his father squeezed out the time and helped. Mike said they were working on the car before 5:00 a.m. on Canada Day, the morning of the competition. His father worked on holidays because corner grocery stores were among the few places open seven days a week back then, and he had to be at the produce wholesaler by six, so at five they were putting the wheels on the car.

The racer had the standard design of most backyard downhill flyers. It was a box on a board, with two-by-fours as axles. The steering mechanism was a rope attached to the front axle, and the wheels had served an earlier tour of duty on a baby carriage. The brakes were the shoes on Mike's feet. And before his father left to pick up his milk and eggs and vegetables, he gave Mike something else. It was a pair of swimming goggles, one of the many things that his father just happened to have. "It may keep the wind out of your eyes."

In his first heat Mike would be up against Ralph. Ralph's father owned an auto body shop, and as Mike unloaded his go-kart from the back of his mother's station wagon, he marvelled at Ralph's customized vehicle. The other drivers were walking around it saying they would be lucky to get into his slipstream. No one thought of beating him. The front was moulded like the hood of a real car. And it was painted—blue, like a real car. Most of the go-karts were coloured the standard factory brown of the wood that they were constructed of. Ralph's car had brakes that worked by pushing on a pedal, which pulled ropes and levers that squeezed rubber-covered wooden blocks against the back wheels. It also had a steering wheel, and a seat with padding. But most scary of all to the competition was the personalized licence plate on the back that read: SPEEDY. Once you say you are something, that is what you become, and that is what others believe you are.

Mike had a licence plate too, sort of. It was a sticker on the side of the box that said Terry's Drive In Market. But he also had the goggles, still in his pocket.

"Good luck to you all," the starter said. He was one of the fathers.

"They're going to need luck," said Ralph. "I'm going to win."

They were at the starting line at the top of a steep hill. Mike took the goggles out of his pocket and slipped them on.

"To keep the wind out of my eyes," he said to Ralph.

"That's not fair," said Ralph.

"Why not?" said the starter.

"'Cause I didn't know you could wear them and now he won't have wind in his eyes."

"Get set," said the starter.

"But I'm going to have wind in my eyes," said Ralph.

"Use your brakes," said Mike.

"Go," said the starter.

"They pushed with their feet and roared with their throats." It is a fact in go-kart racing that the louder you make your voice go, the more "brrr, brrrrr" you put into it, the faster you will go.

A quarter of the way down the hill, Ralph and Mike were nose to nose.

"Brrrrr," said Ralph.

"Brrrr, brrrrrr," said Mike.

Then Mike shouted, "I don't feel the wind."

Ralph squinted. Never before in any race had his eyes bothered him, but now they were burning. "Not fair," he yelled.

The truth, Mike told me more than twenty years after the race, was that he could not see at all. The goggles were made of wobbly plastic and he did not put them on right and he couldn't take his hands off the rope to fix them or tear them off. He strained and squinted but all he saw was a moving blur. He was afraid he would crash, so all he could do was hold the wheels straight and yell at the top of his voice, "Brrrrrrrr! Brrrrrrr!!"

He only knew the race was over when he heard the cheering. "Mikey won. Mikey won!"

He dragged his feet until he could smell rubber. Then, *bang*. The impact knocked him off the board and his hands hit the ground. He pulled off his goggles and there was Ralph's car, tangled up with his.

"It's not fair. I couldn't see," said Ralph. "You had goggles."

"Let's race again," said Mike, "and to make it fair you can use the goggles."

They did race a second time, and you know what happened. Mike won that time too. Ralph put on the goggles and right after he left the starting line, he steered off-course and crashed.

"That's not fair," he said. "Mikey didn't tell me how to use them."

Mike was laughing when he finished telling me the story. Then he said, "And back to that garage and me becoming like my father, well, I was remembering the whole story of the race when I moved the pipes and the spark plugs and the tires back into the garage."

"You threw nothing out?" I asked.

"You never know when I might go fishing again with my father," he said, "and it's good to know we have those spark plugs."

Water Works

This story is about Nancy, who is probably going to make a fortune someday. Nancy is ten years old and she is smart enough to know how a trend can empty your wallet. While other kids were out selling lemonade last summer, Nancy was watching her mother go to the store and come home with bottles of water that she had paid money for.

"Why don't you drink the water that we get at home?" she asked.

"It's not as good as this," her mother said.

Nancy never took a course in marketing, but she is observant.

Her mother is part of one of the fastest growing consumer trends in history. In the early 1990s, bottled water was making little more than a zero percent profit. Now it is a four billion-dollar-a-year industry. If Canada controlled the business, the national debt would soon be washed away.

After air, water is the earth's most plentiful commodity and most people in industrialized countries get it free by turning on a faucet. So the product being sold is not water, but the idea that tap water has gotten dirty. That is at least part of the reason why so many people are willing to pay more for water than for gasoline, which is in short supply and must be nudged expensively from oil.

It is true that tap water is full of impurities and has chlorine in it. But most of the impurities occur naturally, and without the chlorine, those impurities can kill you. Adding chlorine was a major public health breakthrough that saved more lives than you can add up on your calculator. When Jesus was changing history, no one drank water without adding wine to it. Without the wine they could get violently sick from one sip from the well. Chlorine does less damage than wine to a one-year-old. And if you do not want the chlorine, all you need to do is let the water sit for a while and it will evaporate, by itself, no charge.

But it is more fashionable to drink water out of a bottle from a store. And not just any water will do. The number one best-seller in Canada and America comes from France. Evian outsells all other bottled water by a large margin even though France has never been known for having particularly clean water. The French prefer the drink Jesus was used to. Canada has more natural fresh water than any other country on this planet, and most of it comes from nearly untouched and unpolluted wilderness. But the bottlers of Evian hatched a brilliant marketing scheme. Put Evian to your lips and you are touching the water of cultured Europeans, exotic and expensive. *Evian* spelled backwards is Naïve, a word born in France that means "having a lack of social or economic sophistication."

Nancy's mother drinks Evian. Nancy's friends were selling lemonade and Kool-Aid, meaning that their mothers

217

were taking turns going out on the street to buy back their own lemons and Kool-Aid. Nancy put together a need for liquid and a desire for fashion and made a large sign that said: GARDEN FRESH BOTTLED WATER. 50 CENTS.

She took her mother's empty water bottles, all sixty-five of them, and filled them with the hose from the garden. She shook each one to help get rid of the chlorine taste and she tapped into the four billion-dollar-a-year marketing phenomenon. She hired the other kids to abandon their own businesses and hold up more signs, one at each end of the street. It took a day and a half to sell out of water. The other kids went home for more bottles.

She made other signs: GUARANTEED FRESH. GUARANTEED PURE CANADIAN. "I only tell the truth," she said. They sold one hundred bottles in three days.

Their pockets were heavy when they finally went out of business, which they did only because they ran out of bottles. Nancy reported that even her own mother had been a customer, and had said the water tasted better than the stuff she got at the store.

"I know it was true," said Nancy. "It had to taste better. It was guaranteed."

Nancy and Evian are not the only bright drawers of water. There is a company in New York City that is cashing in. They are bottling water from a canal in Brooklyn that has not seen fish or any other life form for a century. The water is filtered and cleaned and is being aimed at a niche market in Europe, mainly France. They are putting a picture of the Brooklyn Bridge on the label, because that is evocative of people who are arrogant and obnoxious, traits the French try to excel at.

As a kind of joke, since all bottled water has to be guaranteed to be something, the bottlers guarantee that no Teamsters are floating in their Gowanus Canal liquid. They hope it makes the buyers laugh. It certainly makes the sellers laugh. Everyone, including Nancy, knows the old joke about those who laugh all the way to the bank, especially when they are banking on something that is guaranteed.

Spitting Image

This is the story of how sunflower seeds may have saved the baseball game, and protected some kids from insanity. It was the bottom of the ninth and Tyler's team was in a deadlock tie with Brandon's team 19 to 19. Tyler and Brandon were both six. They were in organized t-ball. Both wore uniforms. Both had adults watching them and making sure that the rules were followed and everyone got a chance to play and everything was fair and no one got hurt. That is the way baseball should be, the adults said.

Meanwhile, both Tyler and Brandon were doing the most important thing in the world that baseball players actually do. They were learning to spit. The coaches had practice sessions in throwing and catching and hitting the ball and figured that was why the kids were there. Wrong. The kids wanted to be like the major league players on TV, and what they do is spit. That is a talent a kid can cultivate without coaching.

"Yuck," said Tyler's mother. She was sitting in the stands. "I don't know why they do that."

Out on the field her son, oblivious to the game, was

wrapping his tongue around a shell. Out it came, *pwth*, which is the sound of a moving shell mixed with a spray of saliva. *Pwth*. Another shot, but this was a bunch of shells, like cotton candy buckshot.

In this new age of spitting, we can be thankful that chewing tobacco is out, even among big league players. They have learned that life with a million-dollar contract is less fun if the bottom of their mouth has rotted away.

But sunflower seeds, wow. There is the perfect spitting ammo—healthy, clean and you can curl your tongue around one and—*pwth*—fire away. A good shell will go five feet before it hits the ground. Now that is baseball. In the major leagues, umpires have to keep sweeping the shells off home plate or someone sliding in will look like he has gone through a threshing mill.

So far, in the 19–19 game, every player on both sides had gotten a hit. The coaches felt proud. They had done their job. One more inning and the game would be over, and no one would lose, so no child would have a dent in his or her personal development.

The next girl up hit a ball to Tyler, who did not see it coming because he was trying to crack open a seed. The ball bounced right past him.

"Tyler, Tyler, Tyler," his mother shouted. "Get the ball."

"Oh?" said Tyler, who had suddenly remembered why he was standing there. He had been pretending he was winning a spitting contest, but now he had to run after the ball. The seeds came flying out of his pocket while he ran and ran—and crashed right into the centre fielder, who was also spitting seeds and did not see the ball or Tyler.

The two of them fell down and the base runner rounded third and headed for home, which would have made it 20–19 and the game would have been over. That was not good: one team would lose. Still, half the parents were cheering and one of the coaches cheered.

"Wait," said the umpire. "Sunflower seed interference."

"That's not in the rule book," said the coach, who was the coach of what would have been the winning team.

"Doesn't matter," said the umpire. "Seeds were stuck to the bat and the ball." He pointed to the bat on the ground. "You can't have anything stuck to the bat or the ball. It is still 19 to 19."

The coaches argued. The umpire argued. The parents argued. When they stopped shouting at each other, they noticed that the kids were gone. Both teams had disappeared.

They hunted for them and found them behind the stands. Still in their uniforms, they were playing in a game of their own. They were seeing who could spit seeds the farthest. No adults, no rules, no supervision, and most of all, the kids had no trouble seeing who had won.

CANNEd LAUGHTER

One of the great, truly great games of all time is hardly seen any more. And for a change, the culprit is not computers or music videos, it is juice—juice that comes in boxes.

The game is kick the can, a sport for all ages. Eight- and ten- and twelve-year-olds all played together. In fact, anyone who wanted to join in just did so. There were no sides and no size limits. It would start with some kid coming out on the street with a big empty pineapple or tomato juice can. It was a prize; it was almost two quarts big. And as soon as kids heard the sound of the can getting kicked down the street, everybody came to play. Boys and girls who were indoors when they heard the can even ate their vegetables, just so they could get out of the house and onto the street.

The game usually started at dusk. This was not a game for playing in the sunshine, because you had to hide, which was best done behind cars and telephone poles. Kids were skinny enough then to stand behind a pole and disappear. And because darkness was best for hiding, kick the can was an autumn game.

Someone was chosen to be "it." The can was placed on top of the sewer plate, which was home base. Whoever was "it" closed his eyes and counted to ten while everyone else ran and hid. That was potato count—one potato, two potato, and so on—so that he couldn't count too fast.

At the count of ten you had to freeze, and if whoever was "it" saw you and shouted your name, you were captured and you had to go stand near the sewer. But someone else could free all those who were captured by sneaking up and kicking the can. That released everyone until whoever was "it" grabbed the banging, rolling can and ran back to the sewer with it. If he saw anyone moving after he grabbed the can, that person was "it."

The best thing about kick the can was that there was no skill level, no equipment, no expense, no separation of boys and girls.

However, we did have this one problem, called Victor. Victor was the mean kid in the neighbourhood. He liked destroying things. It seemed to be his nature. When Victor played kick the can, he would run as fast as he could to the can, but not because he wanted to free anyone. No, he just wanted to hammer it so hard with his shoe that it bent right in half. These were steel cans, not aluminum as they are now. Victor was not bright, but he was very strong. Once he did that, the can wouldn't stand up any more and the game was over. And that meant Victor ruined almost every game he showed up at.

Except for the night when we all got together before we started to play, and decided to be ready just in case Victor did what Victor usually did. A bunch of us got captured during the game and we were standing around the sewer plate hoping that someone—anyone except Victor—would save us. But out of the night we saw his large, mean shape ripping across the sidewalk and heading straight for the can. He hit it like a football player and almost put his shoe through the side.

We took off running in all directions while Victor shouted, "I kicked the can! I freed you!"

But the person who was "it" didn't go running for the crushed piece of metal. And the rest of us didn't stop in the dark to hide. We all just kept going. And when we got about half a block away, far enough to hide where Victor couldn't see us, we started laughing at him. We taught him a lesson. Yeah, we sure showed him. Now he had no one to play with.

Victor looked around for a few moments, a little confused, and then seemed to realize what had happened and sat down on the curb. I'm not sure if he got something in his eye or not, but he seemed to be rubbing his face.

Then he picked up the can and worked on it until he had it straightened out, and he stood it up on the sewer plate. "Anyone want to play kick the can?" he shouted. He said it a couple more times, and we started drifting back. The game soon began again and nothing was said about running away.

From then on Victor just kicked the can. He didn't try to kill it. The rest of that night was a lot of fun. It was one of the best games of kick the can we ever had.

Now, when I go to the store and see all that juice being sold in boxes, I realize it's no wonder that kids today say they're bored, and that people like Victor end up in counselling.

THE LAKE THAT GOT AWAY

Carlo slid out from under his old fishing van and wiped some grease from his hands and said to me, "Nothing will go wrong this time." He didn't mean his van, which is a mobile fishing lodge that he bought second-hand ten years ago and that he has never washed. Soap would ruin the magic, he says. And besides, the rust would crumble if a sponge touched it.

"Wrong," I said, and I wasn't talking about his van either. "I'll bet you a dollar we come home with no fish." I am not a prophet of doom, but when I go fishing with Carlo something always, absolutely always, goes wrong.

"I tell you this trip will be blessed," he said while tightening the exhaust pipe. "We will eat fish."

Carlo lives for fishing, and like all fishermen he always finds some way of winning. When I am wet and cold and have no fish he says, "Look at the experience you're having."

When he was a kid he dove into the Fountain of Trevi in Rome and pretended that the coins on the bottom were fish that he could snag and take home to his mother like a prize catch. Later he moved to British Columbia and found his heaven in the fields and streams, where he could truly catch his dinner. He talks about fishing. He reads fishing magazines. He plans fishing trips on Mondays after he returns from fishing on Sundays. And this trip to Ross Lake would be bountiful, he said. He would make up for those other times, he promised.

We left after dinner and took the highway east from Vancouver for three hours and then turned off onto sixty kilometres of logging road through the Skagit Valley Provincial Recreation Area. The road was like the ribs of a giant. Every bolt and seat and door, and our teeth, rattled like marbles inside a tin can. Then dust came up from the road and blew in through the rust holes in the floor of the van and soon we could not breathe and Carlo could not see the windshield.

"It will be worth it," said Carlo. "I promise you."

And I said, "I have a loonie that says we will get skunked."

After two hours of rattling, we parked near the edge of the lake. Ross Lake now is a family-oriented campsite with a smooth road and paved parking area. The night we were there ten years ago, it was bush surrounding a fishing hole.

We lay down on the floor of the van in pitch darkness. At 4:30 in the morning Carlo jammed his elbow into my ribs.

"It is time," is all he said.

We got out in the greying darkness and picked up our rods and started walking to the lake. Carlo was ahead of me when he climbed a small ridge then stopped. He looked at the lake. In the morning light I watched his silhouette surveying the scene.

227

Then I heard a rumbling like Mount Vesuvius getting ready to erupt, but this roar had a human voice and it was Carlo's. From the very bottom of his soul came a blasphemy that was part Italian, part English and part unknown. It woke the birds. Then he turned and walked past me without stopping.

"What's wrong?" I asked, but I might as well have been talking to the wind because he kept going, back toward the van.

I stepped up on the rise and there before me was Ross Lake—empty, no water. From one bank to the other it was mud, with rowboats grounded in it. This might make fishing somewhat difficult.

The problem: Ross Lake crosses the Canada–US border and most of it is in Washington, and the dam that created the lake has a hydroelectric plant. Sometimes they lower the water behind the dam and that drains the edges of the lake, including most of what is in BC. Most fishermen know this. Most check before they go. But even so, a true fisherman is not going to let a lake that wasn't there defeat him.

On the way home we stopped for pizza. "With anchovies," he said, "lots of anchovies."

He had won. I paid him his dollar.

THε Old MaN aNd the FlouNdεr

Some say you cannot have sports without trophies. Gold proves you're the best. And the silver on the cup may get mottled and ugly, but you will never hide it.

The last time I was in New York, a city not known for fishing, I ran into John, who showed me his fishing trophy. John is a big guy, an African-American in the correct way of saying it, but he says, "I'm black, and I'm good." He is a janitor and laughs a lot. He lives on the top floor of the apartment building my mother used to live in. He was my mother's best friend before she died.

I walked into his apartment. "That's a mighty big fish tank," I said.

It was almost the length of an entire wall in his living room. The size was pretty impressive when you consider he only has a two-room apartment. Under the tank was a pumping system that could keep a deep-sea diver alive.

"It's fifty gallons," he said.

I knew it was salt water because the metal edges of the tank had corroded. But I could see nothing inside.

"That lump there," he said, pointing to something on the other side of the glass, "under the sand."

I could see there was a lump, and because he told me so, I could tell that the lump was important.

"That's my flounder," he said.

This was his story. He went fishing a while back. He always wanted to go fishing, but when you live in the middle of a very big city that is not so easy. You don't have fishing gear because there is no room in your apartment to store it. And you don't have a boat because there is no place to keep it. And you don't have a car because there is no money to buy it or room to park it.

So he took the subway and then a bus to the end of the line, then he walked out onto a pier and rented a rod and reel and a boat and motor. Then he rode out into a bay filled with scores of other boats. It looked like a parking lot. It was hard to find a place to stop. And when he threw his line into the water, there were so many others doing the same thing that it looked like a spider web covering the ocean.

He sat for five hours, eating the sandwiches and drinking the beer he had brought, and nothing happened. Most of the other boats left. He went from feeling like part of Hemingway's *Old Man and the Sea* to just being bored and frustrated.

"I know you are supposed to have fun fishing even if you don't catch a fish," he said, "but I wasn't having any fun."

Then, just when he had decided to leave, there was a jerk on his line. It wasn't much of a fight. John is very strong, and the fish was only the size of one of his outstretched hands.

But he was surprised at how hard that fish fought to get away and how it refused to quit, even when it was in the boat.

John raced back to the pier with his five-horsepower motor at full throttle to show off his fish. He didn't know it was a flounder until someone told him. Then he took a taxi home, carrying the fish in a bucket of water.

"But you are supposed to eat it," I said.

"No way," he said. John has a voice that falls on you like a medicine ball. You do not ignore it. "I'd be a fool to spend that much on a meal."

"But you spent a fortune on the tank."

"Doesn't matter," he said. "When I look at that fish I feel good. He made me a fisherman."

When you know the value of something, you do not argue about the cost. For that alone John wins the top prize. But there is another difference between his one-pound breathing trophy in a four-foot tank and someone else's stuffed six-foot marlin on a wall. It is that John does not have to pretend his fish still has the fight left in it.

Sailing on Como Lake

I love the ponds and lakes in the Lower Mainland of BC. Most, like Trout Lake in Vancouver and Deer Lake in Burnaby, are less than a minute's walk from streets and homes. Some are stocked with fish and they all have the same rule: you can only throw in a hook if the cheeks of your face are either very smooth or showing signs of wrinkles—nothing in between. To fish in these lakes, you must be under age sixteen or a senior.

But not all the fishing is done with poles. A pair I know managed to bring home dinner using only a memory, a model and a little bit of luck.

It started when Alex asked his grandfather if they could go fishing with the boat that his grandpa was building.

Grandpa shook his head. "No, big fellow. It's only a toy. But you can make believe you are fishing."

Alex sat on a stool in his granddad's workroom while sawdust filled the air and a small wooden boat slowly came to life. He loved his grandfather. He loved his whiskers. He loved his voice. And he loved that his grandpa had been a fisherman, just like he wanted to be.

"Will it look like your boat?" he asked.

Grandpa held the boat next to a picture on the wall of a gillnetter with a man and woman standing on the deck.

"What do you think?" he asked.

Alex's eyes went from the boat in the hand to the boat in the photo and back again.

"Just like yours," he said with a smile.

"That boat was like you and me," said Grandpa, "the best of friends. Your grandma and me ate in that galley right down there," and he pointed below the wheelhouse on the model boat.

The boat in the picture had supported their family, including the little girl who later became Alex's mother. For years, Grandpa and Grandma worked side by side while Grandma talked of the time when they would retire and have grandchildren. Sadly, Grandma never saw Alex.

Grandpa lived alone now, in the basement of his daughter's home, listening to Alex run around on the floor over his head, and loving the noise he made.

Almost every day they went to Como Lake near their home in Coquitlam. Como Lake is a round pond, circled by a walking path. It is stocked with trout.

"All you need for fishing," Grandpa told Alex, "is a good boat, a good crew and a good piece of luck. Your grandmother was my first mate."

Alex knew what the luck was—an old brass button from the navy coat of Grandpa's father. He had seen it and held it many times, and each time it had gone back into his grandpa's pocket.

"I never went fishing without it," said Grandpa.

"How come we can't fish with this boat?" asked Alex.

"It's too small," said Grandpa. "But when you pretend, you can catch anything."

The little boat was battery powered and remote controlled, a special gift that Grandpa longed to give. The day after they painted it, they took it to the lake for the maiden voyage. They packed sandwiches and juice. It would be an all-day adventure. Grandpa also brought his fishing pole, because he always brought his fishing pole.

Alex carefully slipped his boat into the lake. He started the motor and it worked, and man and boy looked at each other's smiles. Alex steered his boat in circles, then zigzags, and he walked along the edge of the lake following the boat.

Grandpa watched him go, and then settled down to an afternoon of talking and fishing with his friends. A half hour passed without anyone noticing.

"Look at that!" One of Grandpa's friends pointed at the water as the little boat sailed past their fishing lines.

"I caught a fish," shouted Alex as he ran back to them. "Did you see the back of the boat go down? I got a fish."

He ran to his grandfather and steered his boat to shore. Trailing behind it was a line tied to a stick. The stick was attached to the wheelhouse with an elastic band.

"Just like your boat," said Alex.

He beached the boat and pulled in the line, and a tiny trout was hooked at the end of it. Alex had used a rolled-up piece of bread for bait.

"He's just like his grandfather," someone said.

Alex beamed. He let the fish go, and then he took the boat out of the water. Whoops, something was wrong.

Something was rattling around deep inside the hull.

"Better check it," said Grandpa.

Alex shook the boat, then shook it some more, and out of the chimney that rose up from the wheelhouse fell the brass button. He picked it up and looked at his grandfather.

"You have the boat. Now it's time you have the luck," said Grandpa. "And I'll pretend I'm your crew."

WOMEN, WORMS AND PREJUDICE

We sometimes learn the most important things from simple events. It was a worm and a joke that taught me a lesson about the evils of prejudice.

It started when a fellow I work with named Mike was laughing about his wife, who was squeamish about putting a worm on a hook. "She just says, 'They're slimy and they wiggle'," he said. "She won't touch them no matter what." He said that her only other comment about worms was: "Yuck!" Mike and I laughed because we are guys and we aren't afraid of worms, no sir. We are strong.

Darlene, his wife, is no slouch either. She and Mike ride motorcycles on back trails together and they go winter camping. She is a tough chick in most everything. But worms? Never.

I thought this was funny, and I started to generalize, which is the seed of all prejudice. If Mike's wife didn't like worms, then probably other women didn't like them. My own wife won't touch them and that made two women; therefore, with the logic of a narrow mind, it was safe to say that all women did not like worms. And because all women had this weakness, they were fair game for making fun of, at least behind their backs.

"You know what women say?" I joked to Mike. "Please put this worm on my hook for me, but don't hurt it." We laughed.

When we went fishing with the other guys, one of them would hold up a worm and kiss it and say, "If my girlfriend saw me do that, she would get sick." Ha ha.

And someone else would pretend that he was a girl and dangle a worm from his fingers and say, "Ooohhh, it's slimy. Ooohhhhhh, it's wiggling."

Ha ha. It was fun. An innocent joke, we figured. It is easy to make fun of a group of people when they are not there. We were just saying what we knew to be true, and it didn't hurt anyone.

The trouble is, it does hurt. When we belittled women, we were no different than someone else saying, " I know this (fill in here: race, religion, nationality, color of skin, sexual preference, etc.) guy. He's like all of them. They're cheap. They smell. They're stupid. They're cowards. They're afraid of worms." We know it's true because we heard someone else say it's true. So we repeat it.

Then one day I made a joke about women and worms with a new woman friend of mine named Tracey. I laughed and said it was funny how women get upset about worms and are afraid to touch them.

Tracey didn't laugh. She just gave me an icy stare. In fact, if looks could punch you in the nose, mine was starting to bleed. Tracey, it turned out, was the senior editor of a fishing magazine.

"It's funny, isn't it?" I said. "I mean, women *are* afraid of worms," I said, more slowly. "Aren't they?"

"No."

"But women and worms *are* funny, aren't they?"

"No. I fish with worms," she said. "And I have many women friends who fish with worms. And besides that, it hurts to be laughed at."

"But I know some women who are afraid of worms," I said in my own defence.

"And I know some men who *are* worms," she said. "But I don't make fun of them."

"You're really not afraid?" I asked.

"No," she said. "I've even kissed a few worms, because underneath, sometimes there is a prince."

I was afraid to ask whether she was referring to boneless creatures that live underground, or spineless creatures with two legs.

A few days later I told Mike, who told Darlene.

"You were laughing at me, behind my back?" she said.

Mike said the couch was very lonely that night.

Early the next morning, Darlene insisted that they go fishing. "And she put the worm on the hook herself," he said with disbelief and pride. She didn't quite kiss it, he added, "but she kissed her finger and then touched her finger to the worm."

"And what happened next?" I asked.

"She caught all the fish."

A Quiet Road

I wish I could tell you this story without words, because that is the way I saw it, and that is the way it has magic. It was a silent movie, played on the streets of the city. It had no script. The actors spoke no words. It was different than Hollywood in other ways: there were no screaming tires, no chases across rooftops, no guns, no adrenalin rush and no exorbitant ticket price.

The city was mostly still asleep when the story began. The sun was opening its eyes. Steam was rising from vents in the street and there was almost no traffic. The only sound throughout the whole show were the squeaking brakes of a garbage truck and two guys banging cans as they emptied them into the back of the truck.

They were not undercover cops or prizefighters in training, not the way Hollywood sees them. They did not come from central casting. They were just two men doing a hard and miserable job that makes life for the rest of us more pleasant. The back of the truck was stuffed with loose garbage and swollen green garbage bags.

Then one of the men opened a garbage can and on top

of some fish bones and crushed cereal boxes was something way out of place, a bouquet of fresh red and yellow flowers. It is the oddities of life that give it flavour. It is the things that are not the way they should be that puts spice into life and changes spaghetti into pasta with peppers.

In the next scene this garbage man took the flowers out of the can with his huge gloved hand and held them up for his buddy to see. Neither man said anything. They both smiled, probably once again acknowledging that they will never understand the mysteries that end up in people's garbage.

It was like the teddy bear they had found a week earlier in another can on another street. They didn't smile then. They just shook their heads because a thrown-out teddy bear looks so sad. But the flowers were different. They could have been props in a comedy. They could have been dumped there by a jilted boyfriend or an angry girlfriend who was in love one minute and steaming and shouting the next. "I don't care what you think, you creep. I don't love you any more. I hate you. And I don't want your stupid flowers." Bang.

They didn't hear it. They imagined it. Maybe that was the way it happened, maybe not. The flowers might have been a hello or a farewell that did not happen. Or they might just have been thrown out after a party, with one last look before the can was closed.

Whatever it was, the flowers have a story that is a mystery and none of us will ever know the answer. It is good to have mysteries, because life without them is nothing but predictable.

Then the man holding the flowers walked around to the front of the truck and took out a piece of wire and tied them up on top of the cab, above where the driver sits, right next to where the teddy bear was sitting. The bear was tied on by a piece of wire so that he sat like a king on a throne where he could see the whole city passing by. The men never said a word during any of this. Many times words get in the way.

The workers climbed on the rear standing platforms on the back and the truck rolled down the street, with garbage loaded in the back and a teddy bear king with his personal bouquet riding at the front, a royal procession, just as the sun rose.

And then that silent movie was over. The characters in order of appearance: two fellows with a hard job, a bunch of discarded flowers and an unwanted teddy bear. They made a beautiful show.

The Rabbits of Boundary Road

One of the wonderful things about the beautiful city of Vancouver is that we are so close to nature. I do not mean bears and deer. They are big, and when they wander into the city they most often wind up shot dead. Our love of nature does not extend to creatures that get in the way of traffic. But when it comes to little things, like rabbits, we excel in care and tenderness.

There is a family of rabbits living at the corner of Boundary Road and Lougheed Highway, a very busy intersection. This family makes you feel so natural, so at one with nature, just knowing we can share our city with wild, unlicensed animals. You can see them almost any day, playing on the grass in front of an office building.

But it was not always so. The rabbits were not always so lucky. I know because I drive by there every day, and ten years ago you could see no rabbits at all. There was nothing on that corner and nothing for several acres around it but brush and alder trees and weeds. Not only was this a waste of potentially taxable land, it was not inviting to rabbits.

Then a film studio took over the old Dominion Bridge

foundry that sat way back from the road behind the weeds and trees. That was good for the economy because the new owners fixed up the dilapidated old building and replaced the broken windows and put up lights and hired landscapers, who made the area beautiful. They even cut down some of the trees so that the building stands out now, and they put lights on it and enlarged it.

But you could not see any rabbits.

Then the government widened Lougheed Highway because so many cars were using it. They were driving on it because they have moved here, just as I did, because it is such a beautiful, natural city. More trees were cut down to make room for the road.

But you still could not see any rabbits.

Then Home Depot opened a megastore alongside the movie studio, which was good for the economy. They turned some of that wasteland of grass and swamp into a productive taxpaying area.

But you still could not see any rabbits.

Then more trees were cut down and an Earl's Restaurant went up in their place. It is a very good restaurant. And then a chicken and ribs eatery was built next door. This is necessary because many cars are stuck in traffic on the Lougheed because it is still not wide enough, but at least now the drivers have a place to eat when they cannot get home in time for dinner.

But you still could not see any rabbits.

Then more trees came down. In fact, all the trees were cut down to make room for a new industrial park. Lots of asphalt was put down to make parking spaces for the people working in the park. It is nice to work in a park, even if the only plants are in pots on the secretary's desk. But it is good for the economy and the restaurants were busy and the hardware store was busy.

But still no rabbits.

Finally, in the last open space left along the road, a giant new motel was built. This is good for all of us: lots of cars using lots of gas and lots of people spending a night in a bed where there had once been a forest. That is also what it finally took to help nature. We can be proud because now you can see the rabbits. They are right out in the open along a strip of grass next to Boundary Road. It is the last piece of grass there, so you cannot miss seeing them. The grass is only about ten feet wide, which seems to be all the room they need because they play there and hop around and watch the cars go by. A gardener put in some manicured shrubs next to the grass and those are excellent for the rabbits to hide under to sleep, and the noise of the traffic does not seem to bother them.

The way I see it, if it were not for us fixing up that useless land, the rabbits would not have such a nice home. They probably would not even be there.

GatHer AROUNd tHe CAN

Valentine's Day is annoying. So are Mother's Day and Father's Day. They are plots by stores and card companies to get us to part with our money, after which we have to go to our mothers and fathers and lovers and ask to borrow more because we are broke, and then they do not like us so much. It is a vicious cycle.

But there is a way to fight back. It was dreamed up by a friend of mine named John Chant. He is a news cameraman who knows his way around riots and fires, but more than that he is a genius when dealing with ordinary problems. He has conquered the holiday expense syndrome by creating his own holiday. It is a day with meaning, and it costs nothing.

John speaks German and he calls his holiday Abfellfest. In German, *abfell* means "garbage"; *fest* means "festival." Hence, Abfellfest is the Garbage Festival.

John says he convinced his kids when they were small that Abfellfest was fun, and it became a big day in his house. "Look," he said to them, "the neighbours are all doing it. This is the day they come out of the house and say hello to each other. In many neighbourhoods, that's the only time they see each other. Sometimes you might even hear them say, 'Good morning.'"

Anything that brings people that close together should be given a chance.

Abfellfest starts early in John's house. Before breakfast, the kids go through the closets looking for something to throw out.

"Hey, I've got an old shirt," says one.

"No, that's mine. I saw it first."

You think finding presents under a tree once a year is exciting? John's kids get to hunt under the bed every week. Getting a box with terrible socks in it on Christmas morning is one thing; discovering one of those socks six months later and getting rid of it is quite another. That is what you wanted to do when you got them, and now you can do it, with everyone's blessing.

Most of the Abfell stuff is collected during the week in a big Abfell can, which the kids have to haul back from the sidewalk. John said he used to give them a round of applause while they were dragging it in.

"Right on! Great!" he shouted. "You are Abfell champs!"

There is not much difference between Abfellfest and an official holiday. It is a prescribed regular day that is marked on the calendar. It brings people together. It gives them a sense of tradition. Even better, you don't have to buy any cards or wrap any presents, making it a perfect holiday uncontaminated by commercialism.

But John is careful not to let too many people know about this. Can you imagine what would happen if it caught on and became trendy? Pre-Abfell parties. Abfell sales in Abfell stores. Abfell key chains and Abfell candy. There would even be sales of prepackaged Abfell so that you would not have to gather it and wrap it yourself before you threw it out on Abfell Day. Then we would need a Post-Abfell Day to rest before the Abfell clearance sales.

Soon people would be saying, "Abfell isn't like it was in the old days. It was simple then. We used to just gather around the can and toss things out in the old-fashioned way. That's when Abfellfest meant something."

So, a cautionary warning: enjoy Abfell Day very quietly. When you put out your Abfell, don't let your neighbours know you are having fun. Keep the joy of your discards in your family. Most of all, don't let commercialism spoil your Abfell. That would be a stinker.

Beggar, Thief or Artist

The streets are crawling with beggars, and most of them are losers. They want the dollar that is in my pocket and in return for it they offer me nothing. But there is one beggar I cannot help admiring.

His name is Tom. I met him a few years ago. He was not sitting down on the sidewalk with his hat out. He didn't even beg. He was travelling through Vancouver. He had been on the road for a long time and someone had swiped the last of his money just the night before and he needed only enough for a bus ticket to Calgary. Just enough for him and his dog. It was a good-looking dog, one of those mixed German shepherds that are almost white, one that looked as though it enjoyed being petted more than sinking its teeth into someone's flesh.

Tom wore a cowboy hat. On his back was a big knapsack, so you could tell he really was travelling. Clean-shaven face, clean clothes. His dog was well cared for. Obviously the guy didn't let him go hungry, and you like a guy who cares about that. The dog sat by his side with only a piece of rope around his neck.

Tom told me his story, just as he had told others before I walked by. This was on Robson Street, near Denman in Vancouver's West End, where most people passing by had more than a few spare dollars on them. Poor guy, cheated out of a bus ticket. His story was so plain and so honest I gave him two dollars.

Then I watched him for a while, from about twenty yards away. He got a few dollars from one person, and a dollar from another. And five from someone else. I started adding it up. Eight, ten, twelve dollars—in fifteen minutes. Not bad. Especially when it was just for a bus ticket and he didn't have to share any of it with the government.

He went on like this for five or six hours a day, pulling in thirty to forty dollars an hour. The other beggars who sit in the same spot day after day asking for spare change barely pull in ten dollars for the entire day. But what they don't have is the insight of Tom the beggar. If he were running the government, the country would have no debt. If he invested in stocks, he would have bought Microsoft when it was ten cents. Instead, he chose begging.

I did not know that when it occurred to me that he would make a nice television story. It would be his own story of hard luck and how he overcame it, a guy travelling across Canada who was stopped because a thief had taken his money, but who would now have enough to travel on in less than a day.

"No, please. Don't take my picture," he pleaded. It would ruin his life, he said.

"Why?" I asked.

There was a long pause. Then he told his story. His other story.

He had started in Toronto ten years earlier. Different dog, different knapsack, but the same missing bus ticket. On that story he married and supported his wife and later two children and kept the dog in healthy food. That story also paid his mortgage.

Then his wife and kids wanted to move to Vancouver because the weather is better. So he sold his house in Toronto and bought another one here. And as he had done for ten years, he got up in the morning and took the collar with the licence on it off his dog and tied a rope around his neck. He put a pillow in the knapsack because it weighed nothing but it made the knapsack look full. And he put on a cowboy hat because everyone likes cowboys, he said. Then he drove downtown, parked his car a block from where he would be working, and turned into a small businessman.

When I met Tom, he was in his late thirties. He said he would be able to retire before he was fifty. He was making on average $50,000 a year in take-home pay. That was like earning at least $80,000 if he had been working in a place where he had to pay taxes.

And if you happened to cross the street to avoid him, you would walk by his tenant, who lived in his downstairs suite and who was working that sidewalk. Same story, same type of knapsack with a pillow inside, but a smaller dog—so he didn't make quite as much.

I haven't seen Tom for a year. I think he has moved on, or retired early. Or maybe he is teaching a business course at Harvard. He is an actor, a swindler, a thief, a liar and a tax cheat. But we all have faults. On the other hand, in the art of begging, he is a creative genius. And since you usually get what you pay for, when you slip a dollar into his hand you get a beautiful performance—and a version of the truth that you can afford.

The Envelope, Please

The Academy Awards are coming up because they are always coming up so that we will keep going to the movies. It is a plot to get us to give more money to the stars who live the rich, luxurious, exciting lives we all want but cannot afford.

But just as Hollywood is pretend, let us pretend to have an awards show for the people who make a movie real. Let us give an Oscar to the extras.

They are the ones who make those bars and beaches and battlefronts come to life. But while the stars get the focus and the lighting, the background characters get only abuse. They stand under umbrellas or sit in their cars for hours before they are directed to do something. They don't get any credits. In fact, no one even calls them by name.

"Hey, you extras, come over here."

They are moved to a spot and told, "When the star comes out of the door of the house, you cross the street. And look natural, for heaven's sake."

These are the people you see getting soaked in the rain when the FBI agents race by in a car. They are the ones squeezed into the lower decks of the *Titanic*. They are there for just ten frames of film, and they are about to die. They should get an Oscar just for tugging at your heart in less than half a second. It takes the stars three hours to do the same thing.

And there should be a special category for the extras who are most forgiving of a star. When *Rocky III*, or *IV*, or whatever it was, was being filmed in the Aerodrome, it was the middle of summer but the scene was supposed to take place in Russia, in the dead of winter. So all two thousand extras were told to wear their heaviest coats and hats.

Then the director closed the doors and turned off the air conditioning. Two thousand people began to sweat, then they sweated some more. The place was kept warm so that when Sylvester Stallone got into the ring for a few brief minutes, he would be sweating and look as though he had been in a long, gruelling fight. Meanwhile, the extras were soaked under their wool coats. An Oscar for tolerance for each of them.

But the chief of all Oscars for extras should go to a man in Vancouver named Geoff, who was told to cross the street just as the star pulled up and got out of his car.

First, a little background on Geoff. He survived the British Merchant Navy in World War II. He ducked torpedoes. He knows about living dangerously.

Now back to the movie. Cameras. Action.

The car pulled up. The star got out. But Geoff didn't move.

"Cut! What's wrong with you?" shouted the director.

"The light said don't walk," replied Geoff.

"What do you mean, 'the light'?" screamed the director. "I'm in charge here, not the g*dd*mn light."

"I have to obey the law," said Geoff, "and it would look wrong if the car pulled up and I crossed against the light."

The script supervisor laughed, then agreed. The cinematographer nodded. The director turned red, then shouted, "Okay, again, this time with the, with the . . ." He had trouble getting it out. "With the light."

Geoff's part in the scene lasted one and a half seconds, about the average for an extra. But in that flash there was greatness. No one watching the film would know they were seeing someone standing up for what was right, against overwhelming odds. He even looked both ways before he stepped off the curb. It wasn't called for in the script, but he was a natural: a real pedestrian, setting the scene for the star.

Of course, the big actors will still get the awards and make those silly speeches at the ceremony. But the Oscar for the best crossing-of-the-street should go to Geoff, who not only made the star shine, he also single-handedly kept Hollywood law-abiding.

The Clown and the Cake

The trouble was, the ice cream cake was on sale. It was only $5.99 and it had a clown on top, and the sale was in this store only. How could I pass up an opportunity like that? If it had been $7.99, I would have walked on by, but at $5.99, how do you say no to an ice cream cake, especially one that has red and blue sprinkles on it, and a happy face on the clown?

It was almost midnight when I saw it and they were not going to keep this thing another day. I had not bought an ice cream cake for at least twenty years, maybe more. And as I stood there looking through the frosty window of the frozen food display, I had this urge.

I had been sent to the store to get raspberry vinegar so my wife Valerie could make a new kind of salad dressing. She is a sergeant major when it comes to ingredients. Regular vinegar would not do. Vinegar to which raspberry juice was added would not do. She wanted raspberry vinegar, and I knew my orders. "You leave ingredients out and you are tampering with a natural science," she says. "And I won't be responsible if your tongue falls off."

Every week she makes something different for Sunday dinner. It's sort of a hobby. She borrows cookbooks from the library that instruct her in the use of exotic spices, or she cooks a vegetable that I have never heard of and that has spines and bumps sticking out. "You taste it first—and don't be afraid," she always tells me. It's her way to keep the boredom out of eating. She likes things that she can point to behind the counter in Chinatown or the Punjabi market, which have no English translation.

"Look at what I brought for dessert tomorrow," I said when I got home with the raspberry vinegar and the ice cream cake.

She looked. She frowned. "Are you having a children's birthday party?" she asked.

"It's for us," I replied. "After the raspberry vinegar and goat cheese and bread with walnuts and celery, after that we can have a little old-fashioned ice cream cake with a clown on top and sprinkles."

"You're so adventurous," she said.

She poured the raspberry vinegar over the salad to marinate and we went to bed. The next day I warned her to save room for the ice cream cake. Well, the salad with the vinegar was zippy, and biting into bread with celery and walnuts and poultry seasoning was like jumping into a cold lake: it is a shock, then you go back for more. My wife says eating like this is more exciting than going to a movie, and you remember it longer.

But I was thinking of the clown. I remembered that on my tenth birthday I had an ice cream cake. There were a bunch of kids and we all screamed, "Ice cream cake. Wow!"

It wasn't very original, but we meant every word. First you dipped your fork into the soft, delicious outer covering, and then there was a slightly firmer inner layer, which always broke the fork because it was plastic.

All the layers tasted the same, but it was different than eating a bowl of ice cream, which is OK for average days. To have the ice cream shaped like a cake was a treat you only got once or twice a year at birthday parties.

My wife knew what was on my mind. "Don't even think about it till you finish your dinner," she said.

So I ate. I told her the raspberry vinegar was delicious and she was a genius for using it. "Now can we have dessert?" I pleaded.

"Not till we clear off the table."

Finally I was allowed to slice the cake. It felt wonderful. You don't put a knife through a bowl of ice cream. You only do that with an ice cream cake.

Then I took the first bite—but something was missing. No sound of kids. No plastic forks. "It's not the same," I said. "It doesn't taste as good as I remember."

My wife looked at the cake. "You numbskull," she said, "you forgot something." And she began singing, "Happy birthday to anyone, happy birthday to anyone"—and suddenly there was a flavour in the cake I hadn't tasted before.

"You can't leave ingredients out," she said. "Every clown knows that."

The Truth About America

On July first, many Canadians gather to watch fireworks and feel proud of their country. And on July fourth, many Americans do the same. Many are absent from both events because they celebrate their nations' birthdays by shopping across the border. Canadians go to America because it is supposed to be cheaper. Americans come here because, "How much is that in real money?"

So that you can understand them better, I'd like to give you an insider's view on the American mind and on American history, which was created by that mind. I speak as a person who was raised under the American flag, and it is a grand flag because God created America. That was on the morning of the first day, before he created the rest of the world. I learned that in grades one, two and three. I also learned that God said, "America is the finest piece of work I'll ever turn out." He then let Henry Ford invent the other countries.

The next significant event in world history was when Columbus discovered America and made the Statue of Liberty so that others could find their way there.

The pilgrims were the first people to get green cards,

and all Americans alive today can trace their ancestry back to them. As soon as they got to America, the pilgrims built motels and opened McDonald's and Kentucky Fried Chicken outlets to ensure that all future Americans would have places to sleep and eat. That was followed by the invention of Thanksgiving, the wheel, and democracy.

The next big event in American history was the birth of Abraham Lincoln, who, as everyone knows because there are pictures of it in all the history books, was born in a log cabin. Since then all Americans who have achieved fame and greatness have been born in log cabins. This includes Presidents Kennedy, Clinton, Bush and Bill Gates, who owe their success in life to their humble beginnings. All great Americans continue to be humble. This includes Mike Tyson and Madonna, both of whom were born in log cabins.

We then move on to World War I, which was won by America, and World War II, which was also won by America. Both wars were won single-handedly but America allowed Canada, England and Russia to join in because Americans like to share everything.

Americans then invented hot dogs, Disneyland, Coca Cola and television, all of which were shared with the world because Americans believe everyone, no matter how poor they are, should have access to the good things in life, especially theme parks. Cottage industries sprang up, including those based on the invention of cars, air-planes, all drugs and medicines, and comic books. Later, after Americans discovered electricity, they invented video games.

In addition to the big wars, Americans have saved the world occasionally with piddling conflicts. They sent the marines to rescue Grenada, El Salvador and the entire Middle East and Cuba. The Marines, you should know, are the finest Americans of all, after John Wayne. The incorrect belief that some of these countries are still not saved in the American way is due entirely to a slanted media.

I attest that all of the above is true, and you will never find an American who would disagree. However, after living almost half my life in Canada, and having read Canadian newspapers and history books, I have learned that the centre of the universe may not actually be where most Americans think it is. It may, in fact, be just slightly to the north.

Tips From a Shark

I was having an argument with my friend Lorenzo. He said he had never broken a New Year's resolution. I said he was full of baloney.

He said he has a secret, which he learned in the pool halls of the world. He is very good at pool, but I was thinking that his head was a bit inflated when it came to other things, like resolutions. Everyone breaks resolutions. He told me I should come with him to a pool table, and he would explain.

He chalked his cue and asked what I had promised myself last year. He was serious in his question.

First off, I told him, I had resolved to max out my RRSP.

"And?" he asked as he put the six-ball in a corner pocket.

"I really wanted to," I said, "but I ran out of money."

Next he sank the four-ball in a side pocket in a shot that was almost impossible. I could have done that too, I thought, if my arms were made of rubber.

"And I promised to learn French," I said.

"So speak," he said as he nudged the two-ball into a pocket.

"Well, I got the tapes and books," I said, "but I ran out of time." And while I was confessing, I added that I had promised myself to lose some weight.

He looked at my stomach and smiled.

"I ran out of resolve," I said.

When I finally got a chance to shoot, I tried to bank the ten-ball off the eleven. It would have been an impressive shot if I'd made it.

"So, big shot, what did you resolve?" I asked.

"One: to keep my Swiss Army knife sharp. Two: not to believe anything on the news. And three: to open the window in the morning and take a breath of fresh air."

"What!? That's cheating," I said. "Anyone could do that."

He slid his cue between his fingers and put away another ball before speaking.

"After a lifetime at these tables I have learned a couple of things," he said. "One: you should never take a shot you can't make."

There was a click, and he sank another ball. "And two: you see all those people wasting their lives doing this?"

He pointed to the clientele staring at the tables, most of whom looked like the type you would not lend money to.

"They keep promising to leave," he said, "then they come back. I learned from them not to make a promise you don't really want to keep."

"But your promises are small potatoes," I protested. "You get nothing from them."

Then he told me about the time he was at a party and a woman said the label on her dress was driving her nuts. He took out his Swiss Army knife and removed the offending tag. His eyes twinkled. "I'm glad it was sharp. She said I was wonderful.

"As for news, you know nothing is ever as bad as they say, so why believe them to begin with? And the morning air makes me feel good."

He pointed to the corner pocket. "Eight-ball in there.

"Let me add up your score," he said. "You had good, top-shelf resolutions, but you still have no money, you still don't speak French and you're still . . ." He tapped my protruding belly with his cue stick.

He racked the balls again. "With mine I got a date . . ." He paused, a long pause, and smiled. "And the news at night no longer ruins my sleep. And in the morning I have fresh air and I listen to the birds."

He broke, scattering the balls over the table. Only one went in, but it didn't matter; I knew he was so far ahead I would never catch up.

Just a Little Strip of Paint

I have a warning for anyone who is thinking of home renovations, although anyone who has lifted a hammer inside a kitchen knows this already: no matter how simple an idea you start with, you will end up with disaster. Period.

Example: my wife Valerie said, "Would you put some white paint along the edges of the front stairs so we can see them at night?" There are four steps, made of concrete, and the edges are hard to see. Bushes grow on both sides, so it is a stairway in the shadow of darkness. "Just a little strip of white paint," my wife went on, "and maybe our friends wouldn't be afraid of breaking their legs when they come to visit."

She had been asking me to do this for several years, but I knew the warning about home renovations, so I ignored her requests and our friends' safety, and left the steps unpainted.

However, one insane day I decided to surprise her. I went into the garage and found an old can of white paint. It was so old that the top half inch of it was solid. So I punched a hole through the dried layer with a screwdriver and stirred what was under it. Conservationists would have applauded me: home improvement without waste.

I didn't have a paintbrush. The last one had dried so hard that I ended up using it as a garden spade. So I decided to use a rag. It was a small job and I figured I could paint just as well with that.

I dipped the rag in the paint and tried to run it along the step in a straight line. That's when I learned why painters use brushes. The paint started running down the steps, and when I wiped it with the rag, it smeared. But there was a solution. If a strip of paint makes stairs safer, then painting the entire staircase would ensure the ultimate safety. I poured the paint over the steps.

"You did what?" a friend of mine said. "That's too much paint, and second of all you can't paint concrete in the winter. It'll never dry."

"It wasn't raining the day I painted," I said.

But it didn't matter, because I was finished. I propped up a broom handle across the steps, hung on a sign that said Wet Paint, and went in the house through the back door.

Later that day I found a newspaper lying on the steps at the front door, and the pathway leading up to the steps had dozens of round white spots on it, about the size of a quarter, like the pattern on the soles of expensive runners. I called the newspaper and said I would impale their carrier if I found him. They said they would speak to him. Then I went out and scrubbed away the spots.

The next morning, more spots. The same kind. I called the newspaper again. They apologized, again. Then I went outside to scrub. But this time I had my glasses on and I could see better. The spots had clearly not come from the bottoms of runners. They were paw prints, made by a cat.

I called the newspaper back and apologized. Then I scrubbed the walkway.

By the third day my wife noticed what I was trying to pretend wasn't true. "The stairs are still wet," she observed.

"Well, it's winter," I said, trying to sound like a person who knows about paint and weather.

In fact, the stairs were still covered with mini-puddles of paint. I tried drying them with a hair dryer, then with a fan. Then it started to rain. I put a sheet of plastic over the steps, and the rain flowed nicely on top, as well as underneath the cover.

After six days of carrying groceries in through the back door, apologizing yet again to the newspaper carrier, leaving a box out for the mail and trying to keep that dry, I finally took the next step in home renovations. I hooked up a hose and tried to wash the paint off the stairs. That is when I found out that some of it had soaked deeply into the concrete and stuck, like Krazy Glue. Some had stuck here, some had stuck there, some more had stuck over there.

Now when our friends go down the stairs at night, they say it is like stepping into blackness and trying to place their feet on small spotty white clouds. It is almost a heavenly experience, if you trust that the clouds are actually sitting on concrete steps.

"All I wanted was a little strip of white," said my wife.

"Oh, is that all?" I asked. "Well, just as soon as I find a can of white paint, and the weather gets warmer, and I buy a brush and clean off the old paint, and cancel the newspaper, and wait until our neighbours with the cat move—I'll get right to it. Sounds like a simple job to me."

Paper Profits

It is amazing how human beings, currently the brightest species on earth, just can't quite figure out what is right in front of our eyes.

I was reminded of this fact when a fellow who teaches time management told me that officially, statistically and absolutely truly, the average person in every office across North America spends twenty minutes a day looking for pieces of paper he or she has just put down. Now, twenty minutes may not seem like much. But that's more than half a day a month. If we carry on with the math—remembering that this is not hypothetical, it is fact—we will find that the employee spends six full working days a year looking around on a desk to find a note that was just put down on that desk.

The irony of this is that twenty years ago, people spent only five minutes a day looking for lost paper. But then, that was before the paperless office. You have heard of that. You haven't seen it, no one has, but you have heard of it. The computer was supposed to eliminate the need for paper. You would just write an electronic message to someone else and they would electronically read it and then electronically dispose of it or file it in an electronic filing cabinet, which is so efficient that it can hold not millions, but billions of electronic notes. Weren't we lucky.

And boy, wasn't it fun to write a note to someone at the other end of the office? Gone were the days when you had to get up and talk to them, or even phone them. No, a note on a computer screen is so much more official, and easier, and modern.

The result is that at Microsoft, which has played a major role in inventing and promoting this efficiency, the average executive now gets 140 electronic messages every single day. And the result of that is the executives have little time to do anything but read their messages. At two minutes per message, reading them takes four and a half hours a day. Then there is the answering, filing and disposing. Four more hours and it's time to go home. Most of the messages, it turns out, are follow-ups to previous messages that somehow have been lost or ignored.

Trying to solve that problem brings us back to the problem with paper. According to my friend Dean, the time management fellow, most of the paper in the paperless office is not from the photocopier, which would be a logical assumption. No, most of it is from the personal printer on each desk, which is next to the personal computer—because everyone is now printing electronic messages like mad because they are afraid of losing track of them in the computer.

The result of that is that every year since the introduction of the computer in America and Canada, four times more paper has been used than in the previous year. In short, computers now have us paper-trained.

Bill Gates, by the way, started out just using a notebook that he kept in his pocket. That way, he said, he could keep all his thoughts together in a simple, efficient fashion. Which suggests that while computers and email might get all the headlines, you don't actually need them in order to change the world.

Make a note of that.

THE MAGIC OF MOVING PICTURES

I have two pictures on my wall, just outside my bedroom. I have looked at them every morning and every night for a good portion of my life and I know something is strange about them.

They are old paintings of men wandering across Europe with their belongings in a bag and worn-out shoes as their transportation. They may have been tradesmen or adventurers, or, in the modern terminology, hoboes. One scene shows two fellows dancing, while a friend sits on the grass playing a harmonica. The other sketch is of an old fellow sitting on the ground with a book, his back against a fence, taking a break from his wandering. His shoes, with holes, are resting by his side. He is wiggling his toes in the grass.

Each picture is about the size of my hand. I bought them in a five-and-dime store when I was a teenager. I paid a quarter each for them and hung them on my wall, and they have followed me for more than forty years through many houses.

Here is the magic. Every night before I go to bed, I straighten them. That is all. That is the entire magic. But it happens every night. I know they are not getting tilted by movement in the house, because no one is home during the day. There is no daily earthquake to knock them off balance, and my street has little traffic.

There is only one explanation. When I am not home, the fellow leaning against the fence puts down his book. Then he puts on his shoes and wanders down the road. On the way he passes the fellows who are dancing, and they all sit down to talk about the news of the day. They joke and laugh and tell stories. These guys have stepped out on their own. Wherever they are going is an adventure. Wherever they have been is a treasure. All they carry with them is music and dance and books. What else do you need?

Whenever the spirit moves him, that fellow with the harmonica starts playing and the others hold hands and make steps on the dusty road. They dance out of the sheer fun of being alive, and being free. They do this only when I leave them and go to work or to sleep. They live when I am gone and that is how the pictures get tilted.

So the next night, and every night, I straighten them. They know that I know their secret, but the rules of a magical picture are that the subjects may not move when someone is looking. They don't mind waiting for me to leave. After all, they are in no hurry to get anywhere. They have no watches, no time clocks, no schedules, no appointments, no rush-hour traffic, no road rage. What they do have is reading and dancing and music and friends, and whatever their trades are whenever they care to work at them.

Outside of simply enjoying the passing of time, they have one mission in life. That is to remind me that it is possible to live a good life, to take joy in simple things. They try to tell me this in the only way they can: by tilting the frames that separate their world from mine.

Playing the Odds

The art of gambling is being killed by lotteries. I do not mean because it is turning us into habitual losers. All gamblers wind up that way. I mean because the lottery has taken the romance out of losing your money. And if you don't have that, you not only end up with empty pockets but you have no fantastic excuse for it.

The problem with the lottery is the quick pick. It is lazy gambling, it is mindless gambling, and worst of all, it is no fun gambling. In fact, it is not gambling at all. To gamble you need a system, because when you have a system you believe you can outwit the snakes who are taking your money. The snakes know that such systems do not work, but they are glad to let you think that you have discovered a new one, so that you will try it and they can take more of your money.

A system can be as simple as betting on birthdates or lucky numbers. The person who picks them is in the game, consciously working on winning. But if you introduce the quick pick into this wasted part of life, you add mindlessness to your portfolio of fantasy and that is not a good way to spend a dollar. You put down your money but you let a machine pick the numbers for you. That is gambling for wimps and for the uninvolved. That is gambling without thought or action. It is the worst thing that ever happened to gambling, because you are not just throwing your money away; you are doing it without even trying to win.

In the end, whether the machine picks your combination or you use the numbers on the first two licence plates that you see in the morning, you will lose. But if you go with the quick pick, you are losing while the computer is having all the fun. That is not gambling, that is being dumb. The reason it is popular is because the quick pick is not for gamblers. It is for people who want to buy a fantasy. Gamblers know they have to work just to stay out of poverty.

I tell you this because the racetrack is open again and, for better or worse and ignoring all of the ills of gambling, the track is the one place where you really have to work at losing your money. No computer does it for you.

You do not stand at the betting window and say, "I'll put two dollars on any horse. It doesn't matter which one. You choose." No. The clerk won't take your money. He will say that this is not the way the game is played. He will think other things, but that is what he will say. You have to pick a horse to place a bet. And you pick it because it holds its ears back, or because you like its name, or because it is the fourth horse in the fourth race, or because it relieves itself right before the race. That is the most devoutly followed system in the racing world. The system makes you responsible for the choice, and that can be scary. That is why so many people put their money into lotteries instead.

Let me tell you about my system. It does not require any knowledge about horses or racing. You just have to wait, and a voice will speak to you. I discovered it after more than a decade of learning to read the racing form. This brought me nothing but a lot of losers and a pile of used racing forms. Then I started betting the favourites, but the long shots came in. Then I bet the long shots, and that's when the favourites crossed the finish line first. I tried picking the best jockeys, but they had bad days. I switched to picking the best trainers, but there were always better ones whom I did not bet on.

Then one day I was standing by the rail watching the horses parade before the race, and I was absolutely sure that the number four horse was going to win. It had muscles that looked like steel. It had a winning jockey and a winning trainer. And its ears were pointed back.

And then I heard a voice next to my ear. "Number ten is gonna win."

"Excuse me?" I said.

"I tell you, number ten. It's a good horse. Trust me."

Standing next to me was an old guy with his hat pulled down. He also had a threadbare jacket, an open-collar shirt and a stinky cigar. He was the classic citizen of the track.

"How do you know it's going to win?"

"I know. I have a feeling."

Well, that is good enough for me. You do not get that kind of inside information at the lottery counter, but you do at the track. The experts are everywhere and they all want to share their expertise. So I put my two dollars down on number ten, even though it looked a little unsteady on its feet. After all, an old guy I had never met, and who looked like he had not won a race in years, had told me number ten was good.

The horses pounded around the track. I was standing near the finish line, my favourite spot to be when the fans are yelling, and dust and sweat are flying off the horses. And then I watched number ten come along, bringing up the rear. He came in last, and the old guy with the pulled-down hat was nowhere to be seen. The results got lit up on the tote board and the horse with the steel muscles was posted as the winner, proving that I could pick them. It also proved that I am as dumb as a horseshoe because I had not bet on that horse. Why would I bet on it, when I was told that another horse was going to win?

How, I ask you, can you beat a system like that? Sure, you lose, the same as you do with the lottery. But at least you have not let some computer tell you what to pick. You lost with your own brain and will power, and now you also have a new, foolproof system: avoid the old man with the pulled-down hat.

THE TERRIBLE TEAPOT

This is a history lesson not taught in school: it is the truth of what brought about the end of the British Empire. It was not wars or economics or even tired blood. It was not the welfare state or the common market. It was a little thing. It was the invention of the cafeteria teapot, which became the Achilles' heel.

Go back in English history and what do you think of? Tea. That is what made Britain great. Okay, Robin Hood and castles and Sherlock Holmes may have had something to do with it too, but tea was the cornerstone. It was tradition, and you cannot have greatness without tradition. The rich drank it. The poor drank it. The empire was fuelled by it.

A generation ago you knew what time it was when people started to twitch: it was tea time. All over Britain, citizens and immigrants rested and took a few minutes to think great thoughts and plan conquests and royal celebrations while they had tea. And they did not simply have tea, not the way you would have a cup of coffee. The real difference is that coffee is handed to you in a cup. It is a finished product. You cannot do anything with it except fill it with sugar and milk. This is true even of the trendy coffees like cappuccino and latte, which are just upscale ways of paying more for your coffee than your neighbour.

Not so with tea. You have to make tea. You have to prepare it individually for each person. Everyone has their own moment of perfection when the tea is just right, and, like snowflakes, no two tea drinkers share the same moment. Tea comes in a pot, the communal pot, the pot that sits in front of you on the table. It brews in front of you. It changes like a magic potion. It becomes something while you wait. You can peek, you can stir, you can taste, and you know just the moment when it is perfect and it becomes your cup of tea.

At least, that is the way it used to be, before someone invented the cafeteria teapot, that squat, ugly piece of aluminum with the ill-fitting, flopping top and a spout as wide as a prizefighter's nose. That is the curse of tea. That pot and nothing but that pot was the Jack the Ripper of the British Empire, because no one—no one on this planet—can pour tea from one of those things.

The first thing that happened to the British aristocracy when they tried to use the aluminum pot was that the tea ran down the side and all over the tablecloth. Now, how long can you remain an aristocrat when you are spilling tea on the tablecloth, and on top of that you are sober while you are spilling? Then the working class tried to use them, and the same thing happened. No matter how they aimed the pot, the tea found its own route into the saucer and onto the table. It never hit the cup. Conquering the world was easy compared to pouring tea.

If you have doubts, go to a local cafeteria and make some tea in one of those aluminum pots. It will steep and brew, but it will not be warm and cozy as in crockery. You do not put your hands around a cafeteria pot. Then try to peek at the tea. If you do not peek, how will you know if it is ready? But the top is hot and it does not come off, it just flops over because it is attached to the pot. The manufacturers fear that you will lose the top, so they deprive you of the choice of removing it. One freedom down, an empire to follow.

Then try pouring it. Whoops. Your chair flies back as you try to get away before your lap gets scalded. How can you hold onto a world empire if that's the way you relax?

Where is all this leading? To the end of tradition, sadly, because according to the World Coffee Council, there is now more coffee drunk in England than tea. This has been so for more than a generation, the same era during which the empire has faded. When the history books are written, it will be called the era of the cafeteria teapot.

The lesson here is that we should be careful of the little things. The end of castles and empires starts with an erosion of pebbles, like teapots that will not pour and dollars you cannot fold and put in your wallet. Now let us order a tall-double-decaf-two-percent-no-foam-latte with cinnamon and try to figure out what is happening to the world.

WANT TO MAKE
A MILLION BUCKS—GUARANTEED?

Would you like to start a new trend? Most of us missed
out by not investing in designer coffee and pineapple pizza by the slice. But I have something that can
make us all rich, and it is guaranteed because what the
world desperately needs is more trends.

Long ago there was something that almost everyone did
every night after dinner so that they could digest their
food. Entire families did it together. It was called Let's Go
For a Walk Around the Block. But that is gone now. No
one has done it for years. Now there is power walking,
with special walking shoes, and fingers on the neck to find
the pulse rate, and walking magazines to instruct the walk-
ers. (Few today would admit that they do ordinary walking, just as few order simply a cup of coffee, or pizza with
only cheese.)

In the not very long ago days, Momma and Poppa would
tell the kids, "Let's go," and everyone would be out the
front door and walk down the block and around the corner.
Sometimes, along the way, they would nod to other people

who were out walking. It was slow and gentle and the best thing it did for you was to make you feel good.

Then walking became trendy, and with it came sweat-bands and pained expressions, and they said it was better than jogging, and it was the perfect exercise, and you should walk at the rate of seven steps in five seconds or it would do you no good. You either became a true believer, or it could drive you to sit.

And here is where our opportunity knocks: we can market The Art of Gentle Walking.

First we will need a book that explains how it can improve your family life, your attitude, your sex life—everything. With the right kind of walking you can earn more money, because you can get ahead of other people at work, because you will be so relaxed that you will save your vital competitive energies for when they are needed—when you are behind your desk.

We will, of course, criticize power walking: condemn it, point out how bad it is for you. This is the ritual. Every new way of exercising, dieting, teaching, weightlifting or running a government begins by ridiculing the old way. We and only we will know the right way to take an after-dinner stroll. We can teach it in our classes, or with a home study video. We'll call it How to Get the Most Out of Walking Around the Block Without Wasting Time.

There can also be a machine with which you can take an after-dinner walk without leaving home. This will not be like jogging machines, because it will have a different label. We will need specialized clothing, too: the After-Dinner Strolling Jacket with matching pants that give you the fit that is just right for moving ahead.

We will need a guru of Gentle Walking, someone who shows the benefits—meaning a woman oozing sexuality who looks like she is having fun and who is rich. Wealthy gurus get larger followings than poor gurus. And she will share her secrets because she only wants to help others. She is not doing it for the money. She would give away her secrets for free if it were not for the cost of postage and handling. She will appear on infomercials that explain why the old way of walking will eventually lead to death. She does not want to be an alarmist, but it is a fact that everyone who walked in the old way ended up dead. She will not promise eternal walking, but certainly compared to what happened to others who did not walk her way, it is worth a try.

It will also help if you wear her specially designed shoes.

Our motto: Gentle Walking—step right up and open your wallet.

The result: We will get rich.

The only PS to this is: I bet it will actually happen. Someday your super-trendy friends will tell you about a new way of walking that they have just discovered. You will see books on it and celebrities doing it. There will be Gentle Walking clinics. And you will say, "Darn, missed that one too."

But here is another suggestion. You can make big money off the next total health movement: eating the crusts on the ends of a loaf of bread. It is something we all did when we were small and poor, and look at us now, big and strong. It is a secret waiting to be discovered, and exploited. It will be bigger than yoghurt. And if you miss that, I'll tell you about Total Health Through Scratching Your Head.

It cannot miss. I guarantee it.

A Whistler Kind of Guy

Whistler changed my life. It happened one weekend, after my wife Valerie got a call from her cousin, who said she couldn't use her time-share condo up there because of an illness. Would we like to have it?

"Oh, wow!" said Valerie. "Oh, I mean I hope you're not seriously sick. No? Oh, good. Wow! Whistler! Yes!"

"Wait a minute," I objected. "Do you know who goes to Whistler? You have to be young and trendy, and you have to know how to order sushi." I have shoes older than some of the people who go there.

"Pzzzz," Valerie said to me, in her distinctive way of telling me to be quiet. "It will be fun," she said. "A week of mountain air and hiking in the alpine meadows."

On the drive up to Whistler, we were passed by a Porsche, then a BMW, then a Range Rover with a white guy inside listening to rap music who shot by us at the speed of wealth. I know it was rap because I could feel it vibrating on my windows.

A few minutes later we passed the Porsche and the BMW and the Range Rover, which were idling at the side of the road while their owners were getting custom-written tickets from the police. I think that was a very dangerous thing for the police to do, because then the Porsche and the BMW and the $70,000 CD player would have to pass us again even faster to make up for lost time.

Later I found out that you actually have not arrived in Whistler unless you get caught speeding on the way up.

"I got stopped twice," I heard someone brag.

"Cooool," said the people he was talking to.

All I could say when I finally pulled into town a good twenty minutes after the Porsche, was: "Where am I?" Whistler used to be a little village. Now there is an uptown and a downtown and a centre of town, along with thousands of people walking between sky-reaching condos and along streets full of trendy stores.

"Where are the alpine meadows?" I asked a young woman. She was wearing a baseball cap and sunglasses and she was drinking a latte, and she had this cute little tattoo that went from her elbow to her shoulder.

"I've never heard of Alpine Meadows," she said. "What do they sell?"

"It's not a store," I tried to explain, "it's a place with flowers up on the hillside."

She cocked her head and pushed up her glasses. "You mean leave Whistler? Why would you do that?"

I walked down the street, noticing that by some fluke, all the young women seemed to have coincidentally chosen the same wardrobe for that day. They all wore baseball caps and sunglasses, and they all had these cute little tattoos on their arms and across their backs. Maybe they got them to ward off sunburn.

Then I noticed another coincidence: all the guys must have accidentally picked the same things to wear, too. They all had sunglasses and gold chains. And one thing more: a guy in Whistler without a cigar might as well stay in Squamish.

"I can't find any clean mountain air," I told Valerie. "There's too much cigar smoke."

"Pzzzz," she said.

We sat and watched all the people with cigars and lattes passing us on the street, and I overheard most of them saying things that amounted to: "These Whistler people really know about style."

So I decided to get into the spirit of things. I opened the trunk of my car and took out the soiled baseball cap that I use when I go fishing, and I bought a latte and a cigar. I rolled up my sleeves and drew a heart on my arm with a ballpoint pen.

"Whistler's making me into a new man," I said, but I could not hold onto the image. I gave Valerie the latte and never lit the cigar.

Later, driving home, I went ten kilometres over the speed limit—but just for a minute. After all, it is one thing to be from Whistler, but something else entirely to be identified at the morgue with a fake tattoo on your arm. I could never explain that I was just visiting.

Afterword

The seat of higher learning
(and where you should leave this book)

You want your children to do better in school, correct? I have a method that always works. It will cost you nothing, and your kids will not object, and they will—guaranteed—get smarter.

It is a universal truth that the more they read, the better they will do in school and in life. But the reading they do in school, they forget as soon as the book closes. That's because it takes place in school and they have to do it. The reading that sticks with them is the reading they choose. The images and concepts that become part of them are those that they discover themselves.

There is one other universal truth. Most of us do most of our favourite reading with our pants down around our ankles and our naked bottoms hovering over a puddle of water. This is not possible in school, at least not most schools. But when we are half-naked we simply cannot put down a book or magazine. We go through novels with our sexual organs cooled by water. We devour serious news of the world with a bum as bare as at the moment of our birth.

When we are naked from knees to navel we do the reading we remember most.

I have very bright friends who never went to college, but can speak intelligently about any subject from wine to race-horses. The reason is that they have cowboy magazines, stock market magazines and home improvement magazines in their bathrooms. Even if you use the spare toilets in their homes you can catch up on events in the Middle East or get a preview of new clothing fashions. If some of my friends get stumped in a conversation, they excuse themselves and relieve themselves, and when I hear the flush I know that both they and the topic will be refreshed.

The brighter members of all societies stock good magazines and books within reach of the toilet so that they never face a bowel movement without a chance to grow intellectually. All of us are so hungry for something to read in the bathroom that if there are no magazines we read the labels on our underwear, and we read them in both languages.

By using the potty reading room to its full potential, this country can once again climb to unsurpassed scholastic heights. The last time this happened was after the invention of the indoor toilet and before the creation of television. During that golden age Canadians went to the bathroom a couple of times a day just to finish a good novel. Homework was done on time, and letters were read and answered. Also, constipation was rare.

Then along came television and folks stopped going to the bathroom, except when they had to. There were no more trips to the water closet just for the pure intellectual pleasure of it. Gone was the art of stimulating higher thoughts while relaxing lower organs.

It is time to reverse this trend, time to improve students' test scores and make everyone smarter. Start by feeding your children prunes and oatmeal. They are the fuel of intellectual success. You do not need tutors for lagging students, just encourage them to eat granola instead of candy and in a few days they will be running to the toilet. There they will find no computer video games and no cablevision. You will hear them complain through the bathroom door, "Mom, I'm bored."

Then slip a newspaper under the door. You will hear the pages turning. It may the first time in their lives they use paper for something other than spit balls. And when they come out, they will not only have less at one end, they will have more at the other. Guaranteed. They will have thoughts. They will know what happened in the world. They will have opinions. They may even have improved their spelling with crossword puzzles instead of a push-button computer spell checker.

You will not have to worry about the dollar. You will not have to worry about Quebec. A couple of weeks in the reading room and your kids will be inventing new ways to run the economy and the country. And all of this will happen because you got them to use the seat of perpetual self-improvement. It is better than any classroom because even if they are bored with their assignment they can't just get up and walk away.

So please, take this book with you the next time you go for a sit, and when you are finished with your behind, kindly leave me behind.